African American Humanist Principles

Black Religion / Womanist Thought / Social Justice
Series Editor Linda E. Thomas
Published by Palgrave

"How Long this Road": Race, Religion, and the Legacy of C. Eric Lincoln
Edited by Alton B. Pollard, III and Love Henry Whelchel, Jr.

White Theology: Outing Supremacy in Modernity
By James W. Perkinson

The Myth of Ham in Nineteenth-Century American Christianity: Race, Heathens, and the People of God
By Sylvester A. Johnson

African American Humanist Principles: Living and Thinking Like the Children of Nimrod
By Anthony B. Pinn

Loving the Body: Black Religious Studies and the Erotic
Edited by Anthony B. Pinn and Dwight N. Hopkins

African American Humanist Principles

Living and Thinking Like the Children of Nimrod

Anthony B. Pinn

AFRICAN AMERICAN HUMANIST PRINCIPLES
© Anthony B. Pinn 2004

First published in 2004 by
PALGRAVE MACMILLAN™
175 Fifth Avenue, New York, N.Y. 10010 and
Houndmills, Basingstoke, Hampshire, England RG21 6XS
Companies and representatives throughout the world

PALGRAVE MACMILLAN is the global academic imprint of the Palgrave Macmillan division of St. Martin's Press, LLC and of Palgrave Macmillan Ltd. Macmillan® is a registered trademark in the United States, United Kingdom and other countries. Palgrave is a registered trademark in the European Union and other countries.

Library of Congress Cataloging-in-Publication Data
Pinn, Anthony B.
    African American humanist principles : living and thinking like the children of Nimrod / Anthony B. Pinn.
      p. cm.—(Black religion, womanist thought, social justice)
    Includes bibliographical references and index.
    ISBN: 978-1-4039-6624-7
      1. Humanism, Religious. 2. African Americans—Religion. I. Title.
II. Series.

BL2760.P56 2004
211′.8′08996073—dc22   2004052096

A catalogue record for this book is available from the British Library.

Design by Newgen Imaging Systems (P) Ltd., Chennai, India.

First edition: November 2004

10 9 8 7 6 5 4 3 2 1

Printed in the United States of America.

Transferred to Digital Printing 2011

To
Calvin Roetzel
and
My Humanist Ancestors

Contents

IV. Toward the Development of Black
Humanist Studies

Acknowledgments

This project developed over the course of several years, and through the support and encouragement of numerous people. While I cannot thank them all by name, I must thank my wife, Cheryl Johnson, for putting up with me and showing me undeserved patience. While several organizations have demonstrated an interest in my work on humanism, I am particularly grateful to the Humanist Institute, First Unitarian Society (Minneapolis), All Souls Unitarian Universalist Church (Kansas City, Missouri), and the Council for Secular Humanism (Amherst, New York) for inviting me to present some of what is given in the following pages. My colleagues in the Society for the Study of Black Religion also provided forums during which my ideas could be debated. Without the support of Amanda Johnson and the others associated with Palgrave Macmillan, this project would have remained another file on my computer. I am also grateful to Dwight Hopkins and Linda Thomas, the series editors. Thank you. Finally, I want to acknowledge the encouragement and sound advise I have received from Calvin Roetzel over the past ten years. It is to Cal and the ancestors that I dedicate this book.

Finally, I acknowledge with gratitude permission to make use of previously published materials from the following:

Anthony B. Pinn, "Handling My Business: Rap Music's Humanist Sensibilities." In Anthony B. Pinn, editor. *Noise and Spirit: The Religious Sensibilities of Rap Music* (New York: New York University Press, 2003), 85, 86, 88–90, 91, 92, 93–97. Reprinted here by permission of New York University Press. Anthony B. Pinn, "Anybody There?: Reflections on African American Humanism." *Religious Humanism*, Volume XXXI, Nos. 3 and 4 (Summer/Fall 1997): 61–78. Reprinted by permission of *Religious Humanism*. Anthony B. Pinn,

"Of Works and Faith: The New Religious Right and Humanist Ethics." *Religious Humanism.* Volume XXXIV, Nos. 3 and 4 (Summer/Fall 2000): 41–54. Reprinted by permission of *Religious Humanism. Varieties of African American Religious Experience* (Minneapolis: Fortress Press, 1998), 157–183, by Anthony B. Pinn, copyright ©1998 Augsburg Fortress. Used by permission.

Series Editors' Preface

Anthony B. Pinn's book opens up the entire discussion of black theology. The first generation of (male) black theologians (1966–1980) took for granted the existence of supernaturalism or a theism as the determining reality for African American churches and the broader discussions in African American religiosity. Though William R. Jones's *Is God A White Racist?* (1973) awakened the intellectual lethargy of his peer scholars in the foundation generation of the 1960s, his academic assault on the mainstream black church and its theology failed to cause a significant ripple. None of the second generation of (male) black theologians (1980–1995) took seriously the humanistic and philosophical claims of Jones. Pinn, a third generation black theologian, pursues this scholarly development of humanism not only by acknowledging the ground breaking work of William R. Jones, but also by surpassing Jones. Pinn's *African American Humanist Principles* goes where the pioneer Jones refused to venture. Pinn's humanism, unlike Jones, asserts the non-reality of God. Theism, consequently, does not exist. Obviously this theoretical challenge raises questions about the enterprise of African American religious studies and the practice of the black church with its black theology.

African American Humanist Principles begins with a gripping theological and personal autobiography, one that grounds the entire book in a Promethian struggle for human effort over against any superstition or supernaturalism hindering the full capability of human intellect and imagination. On his journey, Pinn emerges out of biblical literalism because it does not survive the existential dilemma engendered by rigorous and critical self-reflection on faith as well as the soul wrenching contrasting experiences that personal and social realities pose to an ineffective, mystical black Christianity. Particularly, why do black people suffer disproportionately on North American soil if there is such a thing as a Christian God who is all loving and all powerful? Pinn concludes that there is no empirical, historical, contemporary, or personal evidence for God's existence. So how can one claim that black religion and the black church have been and continue to be the primary vehicles for black liberation?

Yet, Pinn still argues that he is a black theologian whose subject matter is African American religion. He is theologian and humanist, religious studies academic and "atheist". He adheres to the centrality of religion for the black community but describes how a black theologian does not need a personal faith stance. In a word, *African American Humanist Principles* eliminates "God" in order to fashion a pragmatic humanism. Here we discover the extension of human creativity and the maximization of human potential.

Anthony B. Pinn's new book expands the scope of the BLACK RELIGION/WOMANIST THOUGHT/SOCIAL JUSTICE Series. And it fits directly within the Series' mission: to publish both authored and edited manuscripts that have depth, breadth, and theoretical edge and will address both academic and non-specialist audiences. The Series will produce works engaging any dimension of black religion or womanist thought as they pertain to social justice. Womanist thought is a new approach in the study of African American women's perspectives. The Series will include a variety of African American religious expressions. By this we mean traditions such as Protestant and Catholic Christianity, Islam, Judaism, Humanism, African diasporic practices, religion and gender, religion and black gays/lesbians, ecological justice issues, African American religiosity and its relation to African religions, new black religious movements (for example, Daddy Grace, Father Divine, or the Nation of Islam), or religious dimensions in African American "secular" experiences (such as the spiritual aspects of aesthetic efforts like the Harlem Renaissance and literary giants such as James Baldwin, or the religious fervor of the black consciousness movement, or the religion of compassion in black women's club movement.)

Dwight N. Hopkins, University of Chicago Divinity School
Linda E. Thomas, Lutheran School of Theology at 2004 Chicago

My purpose here is not to provide an apologia for my beliefs or, as some might say, disbelief. (I prefer to speak in the affirmative.) Such a statement is unnecessary and, for me, a request for such an apologetic "disclaimer" would be offensive. Rather, my purpose is to relay my perspective, how I arrived at this point, and the reactions of those around me. By so doing, I seek to provide a personalized sense of the contours—the shape and texture—of African American humanism. In this way, readers gain a sense of the ideological leanings and experiences that guide my interpretation of humanism presented in this book. To capture as much of the personal tone as possible, I begin with my beginning.

My mother says that I was a miracle baby, born to a woman who'd recently had open-heart surgery and who was on a variety of medicines, any of which could have damaged a fetus. There were already three children in the family, the youngest nine years old, and a fourth had died of cancer a few years earlier. Why would my parents need another child? My mother says "God has the answer. Tony was born to be my comfort in my old age. That's what an old woman said when she first saw him as a baby." Needless to say, this perspective on my birth, the youngest of five children, meant a special bond with my mother.

My mother enjoyed church and church activities; she was a born again Christian and it was only a matter of time before I would step onto that spiritual path as well. It happened earlier than some might have expected and my father, in fact, always felt that my mother had pushed me into this church stuff. "Leave the boy alone" is what he'd say. But I don't think that was the case. There was something natural about church attendance and participation that I recognized and enjoyed even at a very young age. And at that young age, before my seventh birthday, this enjoyment of church services involved some listening, but mainly seeing friends, looking through the hymnal, long adventures to the rest room, and the occasional nap.

Church on Sunday was part of what I did—with my grandfather, mother, and siblings at a Baptist church. I was so young when we attended this Church, Trinity Baptist Church, that I don't remember much. I remember what others say happened. Sunday school teachers attempted to jog my memory, but their faces remained unfamiliar to me. All I really remember about those years in that church is the sanctuary and my grandfather sitting, in a very dignified manner, with the other church leaders. And we children knew to be good and not call attention to ourselves through misbehavior.

I was far too young to be awed by the inspired sermon given by the pastor, or the heartfelt selection offered by the choir. It was a time of community, of gathering during which normal time was suspended, daily obligations forgotten, and enjoyment was the rule. *Communitas.* I'm not certain I understood a great deal about what took place on Sunday, but I did like the idea of spending time in the house of a God who loved us and did wonderful things for us. The fine points of black church theology escaped me, but I did get the 'essence' of it: God loved us and we should love God and each other; and all this was worked out each week during a few hours, when we dressed in our best clothes, and fellowshipped.

Even the day I joined the church contained these basic elements. It was a typical Sunday for me, except for the end when I made my way to the altar. I had fallen asleep but what can you expect from a small child when a worship service can be so very long, much longer than a cartoon and usually less entertaining?

My mother and sister, Linda, eventually came across a nondenominational church in walking distance from our house. It was energetic and without some of the drawbacks of the Baptist church we'd attended. The minister was dynamic and young enough to be in touch with what was taking place in the world. My mother and sister enjoyed the service and I attended one Sunday. I fell asleep. My mother says I awoke, after a good game of "find a hymn in the hymnal, close it and try to find that hymn with closed eyes," and I asked what people were doing in the front of the church. She remarked that they were joining the church and making it their spiritual home. My mother and sister had done the same several weeks earlier and now it was my turn. I told my mother that "I wanted to join the church too" and I made my way to the front of the sanctuary. I gave the secretary my name—and had to correct her when she got it wrong: "My name is Anthony Bernard Pinn." After a few comments from the pastor, and a parade of well-wishers who shook my hand and whispered "God bless you," I was a member of the church.

Being young, I wasn't privy to the inner workings of the church, although my family would become one of the leading families in this church. Yet, I'm not certain why this church moved toward an organized and hierarchical denomination, but it did, becoming a part of the African Methodist Episcopal Church. With this new affiliation, our church became a part of the regular circuit with a new minister coming every few years, all offering something different and bringing a series of problems. It was one of these ministers in particular that marked an increase in my formal participation in the church.

Reverend Hudson was an understated and dignified minister. His hallmark was the sermon as complete manuscript—no straying from the written word. I will never forget the one Sunday Reverend Hudson prepared to preach his sermon. Glasses on. Flowing black robe properly positioned, and shoes shining. Everything in place—except for the sermon. As he began to "proclaim the word of God," Reverend Hudson realized that he had the wrong manuscript. Without saying much, he walked out of the pulpit and went into his office on the left of the pulpit, grabbed the correct manuscript from his bag of sermons and moved back to the pulpit and began to preach! He wasn't the most dynamic preacher in Buffalo, New York. But he was organized.

Besides preaching, Reverend Hudson also taught the Sunday School class I attended. I didn't particularly enjoy going because I believed there wasn't much I could learn in the class. I thought I knew more than the other students. My mother didn't necessarily see it that way and so I attended.

One Sunday morning, Reverend Hudson went around the room asking each student what he or she wanted to be. Many talked about being a doctor, lawyer . . . what children typically say. And although I was nothing special, I said that I wanted to be a preacher. Reverend Hudson didn't let that get pass him; he took me up on it and began my training in ministry shortly after this proclamation.

I'm not certain what I thought would result from this bold announcement—"I want to be a preacher when I grow up." Somewhere in my consciousness I must have realized that he might take me up on this. Perhaps I thought this announcement would set me a part, give me a larger role in some type of drama. I'm not certain.

Perhaps I understood, on some level, that nothing much would result from this: a few whispered conversations getting back to my family. But nothing long term. Wrong.

It was around this time that much of my extended family, living in Buffalo for the most part, began calling me "professor" or "preacher." You can imagine what this might mean to a preteen. It provided a sense of purpose, a sense of place and space. Something to shoot for in a world where each person must belong to something, as James Baldwin reminds us.

My life as a minister, a preacher of the Gospel of Christ, was underway. Reverend Hudson gave me responsibility for a good portion of the morning worship service. I didn't preach—no manuscript preparation for me at this point. But I gave morning prayers; prayed over the offerings; lined the morning hymns. There I was, leading the congregation in morning songs. I read a line and the congregation sang. In addition to this, and more importantly, I led the invitation to Christian discipleship. After Reverend Hudson gave his sermon, I offered those present an opportunity to accept Jesus Christ as personal savior, or for those who were "saved" to rededicate themselves to a life defined by the Gospel of Christ. This young man responsible for pointing out ultimate concerns—heaven and hell, eternal life, or eternal damnation—and this was a big deal. For those in the church, there was nothing more important than salvation and as a young man, this was quite a responsibility—calling sinners to accountability and encouraging saints to continue the fight against sin and sinfulness.

I sat in the pulpit with Reverend Hudson. I wore a suit on the Sunday's I assisted with worship. The games were over. I no longer sat in a pew where my mischief could go relatively undetected. I was in the pulpit and my movements were exposed to dissection. I had to be careful, set an example for others—monitor my behavior and ask a central question: What would Jesus do? In many ways, this became my mantra, difficult as it was at times: what would Jesus do? As wrist bands now demonstrate this mantra is popular again, from members of the New York Knicks to school children who attend services on Sundays and play on Monday.

A role model? Me? Not quite, but it was difficult enough being in the spotlight on those Sunday mornings.

This new role would continue for the time Reverend Hudson remained with our church—Agape AME Church. However, things would slow down for me until this new, young guy came to town.

We weren't quite certain what to think about this new minister, coming from Philadelphia and Harvard trained. We'd heard good and bad things, but he was known as a church builder and that's what we needed. We were a tight, but small congregation needing to grow. He was young and dynamic, coming to Buffalo with a small child and a wife.

Things would begin to change with Reverend Fred A. Lucas, Jr., in the pulpit. Young people would flood to the church, old members who'd left over the years would come back, and the curious showed up. Sunday after Sunday they came to hear this young guy preach who didn't use a full manuscript.

Initially with Lucas as our new pastor, I served as an acolyte—lighting candles and collecting the offerings. But with time, Lucas began asking me to give the scripture lesson and provide special readings for select Sundays, and so on. Perhaps I fit the "profile"—clean-cut, orderly, properly dressed, etc. Whatever the reason, I was in the pulpit again—doing the things that preachers do.

I started my preaching career during a Wednesday night prayer meeting. But I gave my first "official" sermon, my "trial" sermon some time after that. This sermon, the trial sermon, is the one used by the congregation to determine whether or not one's preaching shows signs of divine calling. My sermon was initially scheduled for a Wednesday evening, but Rev. Lucas changed it to a Sunday morning. Because renovations were underway in the main sanctuary, this Sunday service was held in the fellowship hall. The room was full of supportive figures and faces, all—I assume—hoping for my success. Like many of my early sermons, this one dealt with the punishment awaiting those who did not come to Christ. I talked about the sinful ways of the world—short dresses, improper conduct—and I called for those who were unsaved to come to Christ. Three people did. And after the service I was congratulated by members of the congregation. The next step was a meeting with the church and the presiding elder, the minister responsible for churches within my geographical area of the AME district.

During that session the presiding elder asked questions concerning my call to preach: how do you know God has called you to preach? What does it mean to preach the gospel? What type of ministry will you have? I must have provided satisfactory answers because I was licensed to preach. My ministry was now underway and although I was far too immature to handle or make much of the task, Rev. Lucas made me one of the youth ministers—a child leading children.

I'd continue this trajectory, working in the church and maintaining some degree of normalcy in a high school, West Seneca Christian, that was far from "normal."

I learned several things from attending this school, among these various lessons was the realization that Christians come in a variety of forms—some of them crude and racist. I also began a more focused consideration of my personae: I knew what I did not want to be, how I did not want to present myself. While finishing high school and applying for colleges, I wanted to be more than Bob Jones University or Liberty Baptist, or Pensacola Christian College would allow me to be. I wanted challenge and growth, but with some security. I also, although I did not discuss it much, wanted the prestige and appeal of an Ivy League education.

When Reverend Lucas was reassigned to a major pulpit in Brooklyn, New York—Bridge Street AME Church—my decision was fairly easy to make. I'm convinced that Lucas was instrumental in getting me into Columbia University and I was on my way. Columbia would give me everything I wanted—a good education, access to a larger city, intellectual challenge, and the security of a church community—centered around the Lucas family. This was a good time for me, much growth, and some clarity. West Seneca Christian School promoted conformity to a warped Christian vision, and at Columbia all of that and more was brought into question in healthy and useful ways. I began, at this point, a move toward intellectual inquiry and hard questions related to my religious beliefs.

I wanted this challenge, but I was far from prepared for it. Prior to my arrival in New York City, I based my response to questions of life on scripture. This seemed to work because I dismissed anyone who did not understand the word of God as the primary source of truth. At Columbia this line of defense would not work. The "I believe this is truth because the Bible says so" method no longer carried any weight.

I remember one episode in particular. I made a friend rather fast because we both suffered through the same introduction to French course with a far from ideal teacher. Based upon this common pain, Stanley and I became fast friends and have remained so. During dinner in the dining room of the Freshman cafeteria, Stanley asked me if I believed in the virgin birth of Christ. I, assuming this would be an opportunity to testify and perhaps lead him to Christ, answered quickly in the affirmative. Stanley asked why and I responded: "because the Bible says there was a virgin birth." Oops. Systematically Stanley brought into question the "truth" of scripture and the possibility of Mary and Joseph having conceived this child in the "normal" way. He argued that this should not make a difference because his birth does not affect the wonderful work Jesus Christ did. Stanley has since then become more devoted to a somewhat conservative depiction of Christ and Christianity than this initial discussion suggested.

This exchange encouraged a period of deep questioning, a type of existential and religious angst. My initial response was to reject Stanley and consul myself by arguing that he was going to hell, but Stanley was a good guy and I could not dismiss him and his argument that cavalierly. I had to give his argument some consideration. This was the beginning for me, some might argue it was the beginning of the end.

Early on, my desire to teach and write was heavily indebted to and reflective of my commitment to black Christian principles and norms—I would not in the process of obtaining education and career lose Jesus. I can still hear, when I think about it, the words of church folk ringing in my ears: "Don't get what the world has and lose your soul; don't ever lose your Jesus." High school years were committed to heeding this warning and making good on my promises to self and community. I'd let my "little light shine," as the song goes. As an academic in training in the college years, this perspective meant maintaining my involvement in the African Methodist Episcopal Church—as a youth minister—while studying the academy's wealth. I went to classes Monday through Friday and on the weekends headed to Brooklyn on the "A" train. Saturday and Sunday I worked for the church, hoping to bring some of my book learning—critical reflection—into the service of committed Christians. I was learning, in the classroom and from friends like Stanley, not simply for my own benefit, but to enrich the church and community.

My sense of religious life still meant accepting Jesus Christ as personal savior; seeking the Holy Spirit as one strove to live a Christlike life; and using God-given talents and opportunities (higher education) to enrich the larger community and the "Body of Christ." In one hand I literally carried the Bible and in the other was my school bag, containing the liberal arts' "Great Books."

I became an ordained minister in the African Methodist Episcopal Church after my first year of college, and I continued this trajectory during most of my seminary experience at Harvard Divinity School.

"So, you're going to be a Harvard man." This was Mrs. Lucas's, Fred Lucas's wife, reaction when I told the Lucas's that I would be attending Harvard Divinity School beginning the Fall of 1986. Rev. Lucas had attended this institution and I'm certain this had something to do with my decision. He was my mentor and I was following in his footsteps, but the reasons for attending Columbia surfaced again with this decision.

I understood the next stage of my life in clear terms: seminary education and professional life as a minister involved in both the "life of the mind" and spiritual shepherding. I would obtain advanced degrees, teach, and pastor a church. I would, so I believed, bridge the gap between higher education (conceived in secular terms) and the church (a spiritual oasis). I dressed the part—wearing suits in the classroom for the first year—talked a certain way, and tried my best to avoid "sinful" situations. And, when I slipped into sin—a wine cooler here, an expletive there—I prayed with intensity. As with college, I attempted to place my classroom learning in the context of my Christian commitment and my goal of Christian ministry. I was fairly successful with this objective. The graduate school life is a leisurely one. I had adequate time to do my church work, my studies, and to raise serious questions in the company of good friends.

One of these questions continues to shape my academic publications and teaching: What can we say about God in light of human suffering? I posed this question to examine my religious life, my academic life, economic, social, and political life in the United States. I saw problems and inconsistencies. Folks in the churches I attended had tremendous faith and hope for the future, so much so that they were willing to embrace and "love" their suffering as evidence of God's movement in their life. "No cross, no crown." This troubled me. If God loves black folk and wants what is best for them, why do they continue to suffer disproportionately in the United States? I couldn't reconcile my Christian beliefs with societal conditions. I could not bring together my intellectual beliefs, my experiences, and the experiences of those surrounding me. My intellectual and spiritual self had to be in line with my existential self: mind, heart, soul, and senses in harmony.

Some would say that I was in the process of losing my Jesus the longer I stayed on that Harvard campus, allowing academics to pollute my mind. I disagreed then and still disagree. Graduate school life allowed me to put into balance and harmony the components of my total-self.

Readings about God and religion, listening to church folk, and traveling the neglected sides of Boston altered my perspective on academic life and my religious feelings. I decided that I wanted to be an academic—one who taught, wrote, and trained those who would concretely transform the world. I would, I thought, maintain some sort of commitment to the church, perhaps working with church journals. But I would devote the bulk of my time to working for change through higher education.

I still maintained that God was real, but thought that humans fail to fully understand who God is. Our minds are much too narrow and small to make sense of cosmic realities. I believed that the problems I saw, and to some extent experienced, existed because we failed to work with God for change. As my grandmother told me: "God has no hands but my hands, no legs but my legs." So, we have a moral obligation to work for change, to work side by side with God to make this world what it should be.

After a time, shortly after moving from the Master's degree program to the Ph.D. program, this solution did not satisfy me. I still wanted to work through the Academy to transform the world, but I was no longer convinced that God was or could be a part of this process of transformation. I could see nothing in history suggesting the presence of something in the world beyond visible realities. There was no sneaking suspicion, no "smoking gun," pointing beyond humanity. There is no God to hold us accountable, to work with us in moving beyond our current existential dilemmas. In the words of Oscar Wilde: "The true mystery of the world is the visible not the invisible." After taking a deep breath, I spoke a new word: God does not exist.

I no longer talked about God (at least not in positive terms), but rather spoke about ultimate questions of life that are not dependent on some type of "Supreme Reality," a "Prime Mover." Supernaturalism had finally died for me. Some raised questions: How can a theologian—I had shifted my studies from Church history to theology—speak without grounding that talk in a faith stance (understood, of course, for my questioners, in Christian terms)? Yet I wanted the freedom to talk about religion in ways that were not restricted by personal belief. The theologian had turned humanist, if not atheist.

I was able to get a dissertation through my committee without losing my commitment to my new perspective, and I was fortunate in that the job market did not reject a "blasphemer, a heretic" such as myself. I landed a good job that allowed me to think my thoughts and teach what I was interested in.

Until recently, I thought I did a good job of explaining my position as a theologian who rejects supernatural claims. I thought I had provided the intellectual and practical grounds for this combination—theologian and humanist. I said there is no God with conviction, yet sensitivity, and thought about other ways of holding humans in moral/ethical "check": Do no harm because all others deserve respect and proper care. I thought my professional life and academic writings made this clear for both those in and outside the Academy.

I knew that there could never be perfect balance between all aspects of life—physical and spiritual, work and self. Yet, I assumed I was comfortable with this. I would pour myself into my work, but make certain that work was influenced by my life—my experiences and the experiences of my community of birth and choice. I was proud of myself for having been so straightforward—making private life and public confessions respectfully consistent.

This was the case until Tatsha Robertson, from the *StarTribune*, began writing a profile on me. She kept asking a question that I believed I had convincingly responded to: Who is Tony Pinn? I had not presented myself with the clarity I thought. Folks did not understand where I stood. They read my books and heard me talk, but they did not get it—"it" being the connections between my professional life and my private life complete with its "spiritual" dimensions. I needed to think this through.

I received roughly 40 letters once Tatsha's article ran. Others received their share, including the Development Office and the chair of the Religious Studies Department. Almost all brought into question the fate of my soul and the problematic nature of my presence in a "Religious Studies" department. (I thank those who wrote thoughtful letters and the administrators, faculty, staff, and students of Macalester College for their encouragement and support. I am particularly grateful to Calvin Roetzel who guided me through the landmines with good humor.) Some went as far as to request my termination because I, as an atheist, must be damaging young (read Christian) students. They could not fathom the possibility of a humanist respectfully teaching a full range of materials without constant polemics against the Christian faith. Yet, I imagine they would have no problem with a Capitalist teaching Marxism (as is usually the case), or a Christian teaching Islam (again, as is usually the case).

At Macalester College I continued explaining myself, teaching, and writing about things religious. I think religion is tremendously important in African American communities. It represents undeniably important cultural traditions and aesthetic patterns unique to African Americans. For this reason I study and discuss the various forms of black religion, yet this does not require a commitment to a personal faith stance embraced by any of the widely recognized forms of black religious expression. I do not find the various "traditional" religions personally satisfying, but they are culturally rich and worthy of intellectual exploration and engagement. I spend my professional days, now at Rice University, researching and teaching these traditions, along with humanist alternatives, because I respect human life and human creativity. After all, as a humanist, my life centers on humanity and creating healthy life options. As a humanist and theologian, I am concerned with life and responses to hard life questions.

Within this volume I make an effort to discuss both the history and the consequences of the humanism I embraced more than a decade ago.

Introduction: An Encounter with the Children of Nimrod

There is something valiant and noble about the stories of Prometheus, Greek god and friend to humanity. I must admit that I am drawn to the defiance, the determination to celebrate human tenacity, found in those mythic accounts of Prometheus's daring. According to some accounts, Prometheus was the creator of humanity whereby he "fashioned them in a nobler shape than the animals, upright like the gods; and then he went to heaven, to the sun, where he lit a torch and brought down fire, a protection" and ultimately the means for humans to exercise various talents and abilities.[1] The theft of fire from mount Olympus resulted in punishment from Zeus. Prometheus was chained to a rock and his liver, which regenerated perpetually, was consumed by a bird until he was freed many years later.

This episode of Greek mythology speaks of a human desire for fulfillment, and its lessons have inspired thinkers who have embraced the mythic figure of Prometheus as a powerful icon and symbol of humanism's fundamental assertions and meaning. Historically, critical engagement with the Prometheus myth has forged an important symbol for humanism, an orientation or model meant to topple superstition and nurture the best of humanity's intellectual and physical abilities. After all, it is through the gift of fire, the story goes, that humans were able to escape a state of physical discomfort and intellectual stagnation. The development and expansion of humanism as a philosophy and way of life extended from this basic premise—the merit of human potential and creativity—and rejected all that sought to challenge this basic assertion.

Humanists sought to help people live responsibly. From the Renaissance and the Enlightenment in Europe to the democratic vision of the developing United States, humanism emerges as a response to a desire to move beyond Christian abstractions to a more pragmatic approach to human life. The goal was to respond to human misery and the difficulties of life in ways that had meaning and that effected concrete existence. In short, humanism responds to moral evil and its ramifications by an appeal to the essential worth and responsibility of humanity for the quality of life.

Nimrod and African American Humanists

Humanism comes in many colors. To not recognize this point is to give sustenance to a stereotypical depiction that has lived for far too long. If humanists embrace a selective presentation of U.S. humanism, they engage in a form of revisionist history. When more attention is given to issues of race as connected to other forms of oppression, one sees more clearly the manner in which humanism has lived and functioned within African American communities. Consider the words by Hubert Harrison, a significant socialist and activist during the early twentieth century:

> Christian America created the color line; and all the great currents of critical opinion, from the eighteenth century to our time, have found the great barrier impassible and well-nigh impervious . . . . [I]t should seem that Negroes, of all Americans, would be found in the Freethought fold since they have suffered more than any other class of Americans from the dubious blessings of Christianity. It has been well said that the two great instruments for the propagation of race prejudice in America are the Associated Press and the Christian Church. This is quite true. Historically, it was the name of religion that cloaked the beginnings of slavery on the soil of America, and buttressed its continuance.[2]

An accurate sense of humanism's basic principles and system of ethics cannot be ascertained without attention to African Americans and the movement toward social transformation sparked by African Americans.

European humanism and white American humanism develop under the assumption of human worth and integrity. That is to say, these two modalities of humanism emerge in light of an assumed value and worth. They develop as the "surface" of Renaissance and Enlightenment confidence. Yet, for those of African descent it is a different story. They are the "underbelly" of the Renaissance and Enlightenment in that the advances that shape these two periods occur in part because of the slave trade, and the overdetermination and dehumanization of Africans. Mindful of this, one can safely say African American humanism is a reaction against modernity, not an embrace of modernity and its ramifications. The "freedom" upon which modernity rests, at least in part, was not meant for Africans; rather, African bodies provided the raw material for this freedom embraced by Europeans of means. African Americans were existentially "fixed" and denied the ambiguity of being that makes freedom so very sweet.

Those of African descent who rejected supernaturalism were not associated with Prometheus and the "best" of the Western tradition of human potential and optimism, but perhaps with Nimrod and the "darkside" of history.[3] Related to Ham, who was cursed by his father (Noah), Nimrod according to the Judeo–Christian tradition was known as a great hunter who controlled a kingdom that included Babel. Associated with the construction of the Tower of Babel—the attempt during the postdiluvian period to unify humanity around one sociocultural reality in defiance of God—Nimrod became a cursed figure in theological–religious circles. He challenged the constructive and technological dominance of God, thereby threatening the cosmic framework of the universe:

> Let us build us a city and a tower, whose top may reach unto heaven; and let us make us a name, lest we be scattered abroad upon the face of the whole earth. And the Lord came down to see the city and the tower, which the children of men builded. And the Lord said, Behold, the people is one, and they have all one language; and this they begin to do: and now nothing will be restrained from them, which they have imagined to do.[4]

Rabbinic interpretations of this scriptural text suggest a "divine" reaction against aggressive creativity, against an attempt by humans to extend themselves intellectually and physically. In this way, Nimrod is credited (or cursed depending on one's perspective) with shifting the human gaze away from the heavens toward earth and human potentiality. Nimrod, like Prometheus, brings to humanity recognition of new possibilities by taking what once belonged to the gods and giving it to humans for their use in the furtherance of their intellect and cultural expressivity. Through his actions, exegetical traditions suggest "Men no longer trusted in God, but rather in their own prowess and ability, an attitude to which Nimrod tried to convert the whole world. Therefore people said, 'since the creation of the world there has been none like Nimrod, a mighty hunter of men and beasts, a sinner before God,' . . . According to the rabbis, Nimrod's iniquity climaxed in the building of the Tower of Babel, an enterprise that 'was neither more nor less than rebellion against God.' "[5] Clearly, from the perspective of those committed to theism, Nimrod's legacy involved destruction of traditional supernatural patterns and precepts.

Early Christian commentators continued the rabbinic perspective on Nimrod. St. Augustine, for example, argued that Nimrod was a hunter "against" God, and hunter in this respect was a reference to his role as a deceiver, oppressor, destroyer, and enemy of the divine plan for humanity. The tower is the sign of this defiance.[6] A similar presentation of Nimrod is available in the writings of other early church leaders who "assigned Nimrod symbolic as well as historical significance. His legendary role as hunter, tower builder, and tyrant made him a consummate symbol of human pride and rebellion."[7] During the Middle Ages, concern with the legend of Nimrod was often associated with what was believed to be his acquaintance with heretical knowledge, an ability to use the natural world to his benefit. The strong epistemological and biological link between Ham and Nimrod that emerged in soft tones during earlier years becomes a much more considered part of the interpretation during the Reformation and Renaissance. Regarding Martin Luther on this point, "just as Ham despised Noah's religion and doctrine by mocking his father and establishing a new government and new religion, so Nimrod sinned against both the government and the church. He did not cultivate the true religion."[8]

Biblical interpretation and legend discussed in Europe were not lost on the American context. Nimrod and his infamy crossed the ocean as tales of his struggle against God littered conversations of eighteenth and nineteenth century North America.

One can dismiss this biblical mention of Nimrod and the ensuing legend. We, of course, are not tied of necessity to the "truthfulness" of scripture nor the sociocultural inclinations and whims of biblical interpreters. Yet, there are historical ramifications of this story and its main characters—Ham and Nimrod—that caution against easy dismissals. The ramifications have been too extensive and damaging for this. The manner in which the suspicion against Nimrod (and Ham) attached itself to those of African descent, serving in part as the theological rationale and justification for the oppression of black bodies and the suppression of African cultural creativity, demand consideration as a means of correction. From the early writings of church fathers through nineteenth century pro-slavery modes of interpretation, Nimrod, as the descendant of Ham, is presented as an African. Therefore, distance from God and denial of the more positive trajectories of "salvation" history are attached to black skin. In short, Nimrod's lineage has consequences for the children of Africa: "Nimrod was black; his grandfather Ham was the first Negro; his father Cush was the ancestor of Ethiopians; he personifies human nature's darker side."[9]

Such logic played well into the desire of pro-slavery Americans to justify involvement in the slave trade. They, with great energy and assumed righteousness, argued that Ham and his descendants were cursed as scripture indicates and Nimrod, the grandson of Ham, was cursed because of his effort to supersede God. Those with black skin participate in the dishonor initiated by Ham and Nimrod, and they must share in the punishment. And of course this punishment was a form of social death that overdetermined and fixed those of African descent, rendering them will-less creatures who must serve white masters. It is only through controlling their bodies, the pro-slavery argument went, that one could control the tendency toward rebellion (against civil society and God) and disorder inherited from Nimrod.

African Americans throughout their presence in what became the United States have fought this warped depiction, challenging scriptural interpretation and struggling for full humanity. One need only think about David Walker's *Appeal*, the public lectures by Maria Stewart, the work of Frederick Douglass, the violent revolution undertaken by Nat Turner, and the praxis of more recent figures such as Martin Luther King, Jr., and Barbara Jordan. Much of their work is clearly premised on a claiming of scripture's liberating potential. And, while the struggles undertaken by these figures have often involved a signifying against white arrogance and assumed superiority, it has seldom entailed an effort to "rescue" biblical figures such as Ham and Nimrod from socioeconomically and politically motivated manipulation. What would be the ramifications, however, of a rethinking of the Nimrod legend for example?

I suggest, while this may have limited benefit for African American Christians who often have embraced a softened version of the legend, it can serve as a powerful mode of existential and epistemological reformation for African American humanists who have long sought out signs and symbols that might do for them what Prometheus has done for their white fellow travelers. Nimrod, when a hermeneutic of humanism is applied, takes on new dimensions of importance. He, to "flip" or signify earlier interpretations, becomes a significant figure in the development of humanism in that he sought to extend human creativity and maximize human potential. Recognizing the risk inherent in such a movement against established tradition, Nimrod celebrates human ingenuity.

Mindful of this, African American humanists might consider themselves, again through a signifying of traditional interpretations, the children of Nimrod—those who seek to celebrate and safeguard human creativity, potential, and responsibility. Doing so, reclaiming Nimrod from dominant readings, allows for the introduction of a new social space premised on a renaming of African American humanists. It entails, then, a reconstitution of a forgotten tradition of human integrity, a type of "subjugated knowledge," to use a popular phrase from Foucault. If Charles Long is correct, and I believe he is, this renaming through an archaeological enterprise of reclaiming lost traditions and personalities involves a reframing of reality because language has its on materiality. Language is charged in that it has the ability to alter, radically change perceptions and situations. African Americans have recognized the power of language throughout the centuries marking their presence in the "New World." How could they, for example, ignore the manner in which the word "negro" was created and used to fix their identity, to limit their existential possibilities? In response, they used language, the power of the "word," to rethink their place in the world and the substance of their being. Manipulations of language through devices such as metaphor, double-talk, and signification, were used by enslaved Africans and their descendants to demand space and to force themselves into the historical moment as more fully developed subjects of (as opposed to objects of) history. The brilliance of African American cultural production from the music of the spirituals and blues, through literary formulations encompassing the Black sermonic tradition, and so on, points to the transformative power of language to re-envision and reshape the content and form of historical existence.

A similar move gives African American humanists intellectual and praxis-related grounding in a history of rebellion against overdetermined and oppressive limitations on human "doing." In this respect, one might say this reinterpretation of Nimrod suggests that once one breaks preoccupations with supernaturalism and unfounded cosmic issues it dictates, humans confront the possibility (although not always realized as existentialists have shown us) of nurturing creativity and potential in transforming ways. It is this quest for a fuller sense of being—for greater existential and ontological worth—that also informs the basic principles of African American humanism. Some readers will find the lack of a hard and fast definition of African American humanism frustrating. A single definition is unrealitistic in that the tradition is experienced in a variety of ways. Humanism outside of African American communities, as countless articles in *Free*

Inquiry Magazine and other publications as well as debates between the American Humanist Association and the Council for Secular Humanism attest, has not rested on a single understanding or definition. Therefore, rather than a narrow defining of humanism, I offer a set of principles that mark humanism within various camps. The presentation of these principles does not remove what can often be a troubling slippage between humanism, atheism, and other forms of "disbelief." But again, based on the lack of consensus with respect to the definition of humanism, it is only natural that some overlap will exist within certain circles of thought and practice.

The purpose of this volume is not to provide definitive distinctions between these various ways of being in the world. Rather, my concern is to provide a sense of how humanism functions based on a set of principles that serve to frame the nature and meaning of humanism. As I have noted in many places, I again suggest these principles revolve around several normative claims or guiding norms that are both deconstructive in their rejection of supernaturalism and constructive in their ethics for living. Readers will encounter these principles in various forms within the following pages, but I believe it important to state them at the start of this project for emphasis and to reenforce their centrality because they represent a consistent and coherent pattern of belief and action that give some shape to a humanist tradition in African American communities. They are:

(1) understanding of humanity as fully (and solely) accountable and responsible for the human condition and the correction of humanity's plight;
(2) suspicion toward or rejection of supernatural explanation and claims, combined with an understanding of humanity as an evolving part of the natural environment as opposed to being a created being. This can involve disbelief in God(s);
(3) an appreciation for African American cultural production and a perception of traditional forms of black religiosity as having cultural importance as opposed to any type of "cosmic" authority;
(4) a commitment to individual and societal transformation;
(5) a controlled optimism that recognizes both human potential and human destructive activities.

Context: Rationale for This Book

Such a hermeneutical turn, the re-capturing of Nimrod, provides an important icon, or central "metaphor" for African American humanism. However, this is only a part of what must be accomplished in order to more fully develop and appreciate humanism within the context of African American communities. Much of the work I have done up to this point has sought to clarify the contours of African American humanist principles through discussion of their historical development and presentation of some of their major spokespersons. And while presentation of African American humanism's historical contours is vital, it alone does not present a "thick" understanding because it is primarily undertaken as an apologetic or an affirmation of humanism's existence in African American communities. Again, this is important work in that many continue to deny the presence, in significant ways, of humanism: Black folks are not humanists the traditional assertion goes, yet a detailed understanding of how African American humanist principles function must be the next step.

This book is my effort to present the inner workings of humanist principles as the foundation for humanism from the African American perspective—its form and content, nature and meaning.[10] I do so through attention to three foundational areas: (1) personal and communal historical context for humanist principles; (2) humanist principles as life orientation; and (3) humanist principles as hermeneutic or mode of interpreting life. The first section presents the manner in which humanist principles develop historically within African American communities.

While some might argue that there is no need at this stage to justify the humanist tradition because it is a given, I disagree. Humanism continues as a marginal and often ignored dimension of black experience. It remains important to argue for the existence and viability of a humanist tradition in African American communities. Furthermore, some will disagree undoubtedly with the attention I give to rejection of the God concept as a marker of humanism. I fully acknowledge that this is not the only indication of such a position, and I am also willing to entertain the possibility that it is not the most significant aspect of the humanist position. That is to say, perhaps such a stance is not enough to label one a humanist. However, what I cannot deny is the importance of this stance for many black humanists as one of the signs of their movement into humanism. This rejection or disbelief is, I should note, accompanied by adherence to other humanist principles noted in this introduction.

It would be difficult to ignore the manner in which this volume often seems to present humanism and atheism as being synonymous. The distinction between the two, if there is one, is fodder for ongoing conversation and confrontation. The presence of this dilemma extends beyond discussions of black humanism and must be noted as a concern. However, it does not negate the intent and value of this project. Rather, it is no different than the dilemma faced by those who try to provide a broad definition of black Christianity: Whose black Christianity? Which denomination? Is black Christianity synonymous with the major denominations? If yes, what about the strong distinctions in doctrine and practice between the various denominations? Lingering questions such as these have never negated the importance of studies concerned with dimensions of black Christian practice and thought. It is also the case that ongoing debates over the proper definition of humanism (and atheism) do not negate the importance of studies such as *African American Humanist Principles*.

My concern in this volume is not the defining of black humanism as a system. I am interested in the broader focus on the principles that seem to guide what various individuals and groups have labeled humanistic orientation. These principles seem to hold whether one is talking about black humanists in the Unitarian Universalist Association (UUA) or in the Council of Secular Humanism.

I recognize that some of what I present in the first two chapters (comprising section I) is open to alternate interpretation. This is the case with any data. Such a recognition does not disprove the importance of humanist principles within African American communities no more so than the possibility of alternate readings of the Christ event damages the claims of black Christians. Furthermore, my goal is not to "proof text" in a way that makes the humanist position undeniable. I am not, for example, claiming that slaves who rejected Christianity were of necessity humanists. Rather, I suggest that the hypocrisy and racism within the practice of Christianity during the period of slavery and beyond, provided the groundwork for the eventual development and exercise of humanist principles. My concern is with the presence and operation of humanist sensibilities and principles. I am concerned with the description of the manner in which humanist principles operate in certain dimension of black life. This does not entail, although it is a worthy project, a fully formed and constructive proposition with respect to the distinctiveness of black humanism. *African American Humanist Principles* only points in the direction of such a project and encourages its development.

With respect to the second category, the objective is to discuss the manner in which humanism is lived, particularly the manner in which it shapes ethics. And, finally, section III explores humanism's function as a mode of inquiry, as a philosophical tool for life decisions. When combined, sections II and III present examples of the ways in which humanism serves to shape and arrange life for some African Americans, and the first section provides a rough sketch of the context for a life so conceived. In a sense, sections II and III demonstrate the practice of the principles presented earlier, thereby speaking to humanism as a way of being.

In addition, this project entails a prolegomenon of sorts in that its attention to the three foundational areas of concern—humanism's history, humanism as practice, and humanism as hermeneutic—frame the basic structure necessary for the growth of African American Humanist Studies.[11] That is to say, working through the three areas listed above provides a rough correspondence to the basic elements of any formal mode of study: datum, method, and theory. Such a field of study is briefly explored in the conclusion to this volume, with attention given to theological discourse and pedagogy.

History, practice, and hermeneutics provide the basic framework for this volume, and both unpublished and previously published articles and essays provide the book's content. Regarding the use of previously published materials included in this volume, it is typically the case that these materials were published using venues that have limited reach outside (and inside) humanist circles, but in the form presented here they provide perspectives that I continue to embrace. More importantly, they were rethought and reformulated expressly for this project. By combining these pieces with more recent writings I hope to give readers a framework for thinking about African American humanism in "thick" and complex ways. By so doing, I aim to push closer to an appreciation for or "revival" of Nimrod's children.

Section I

The Historical Development of Humanist Principles

Art, Religion, and Politics are impressive vectors of a culture. Art describes a culture. Black artists must have an image of what the Black sensibility is in this land. Religion elevates a culture. The Black man must aspire to Blackness. God is man idealized. The Black Man must idealize himself as Black. And idealize and aspire to that. Politics gives a social order to the culture, i.e., makes relationships within the culture definable for the functioning organism. The Black man must seek a Black politics, an ordering of the world that is beneficial to his culture, to his interiorization and judgment of the world. This is strength. And we are hordes . . . .

—*Amiri Imamu Baraka*

From the early years of frontier life, the people who become recognized inhabitants of the United States were ripe for humanist principles. Mindful of this, the history of humanism in the United States includes attention to the Renaissance and Enlightenment, but also figures who wrote and spoke from the rather unique context of North America—shaping humanist sensibilities in light of American sociopolitical and cultural identity. The reframing of life in terms of humanism was not simply a historical movement on the part of Americans of European descent. The children of Africa living in North America also contributed to humanism's historical progression. Individuals from

Frederick Douglass to figures of the Civil Rights Movement such as James Forman rethought black identity and social justice in light of a radical embrace of human accountability and ingenuity. However, it must be noted that humanism's contribution to American life is not limited to the efforts of individuals working in isolation. Black humanist history is also the story of African American humanists partnered with the like-minded as well as those who opposed humanism, but who shared a commitment to the progress of African Americans. In this way, black humanism's history is firmly entrenched in the institutional and intellectual structures of America in general, and black America in particular.

The Historical Contours of African American Humanist Principles: Part One[1]

While many argue that the United States of America is founded upon overtly religious ideals and desires, a legacy of theological and religious contradiction, combined with frustrated movements toward democracy in the face of modernity, made the United States ripe for humanist's possibilities. From the Pilgrims onward the common nation-story revolved around religious freedom and the creation of a "new promised land." There may be some truth to this, but it is the case that less than thirty percent of the colonists who populated this land in its early years were actively involved in organized religion. The land fostered individualism and frontier life, and this made it difficult to provide sufficient missionaries to spread the gospel. "Spiritual" concerns, when present, took a back seat to economic challenges fostered by an unfamiliar and unforgiving terrain.

It is also the case that Christianity did not appeal to some colonists and their descendants, who instead gravitated toward humanism because, as philosopher Corliss Lamont notes, the basic language and documents such as the Declaration of Independence used to frame life "gave resounding affirmation to the social aims of Humanism when it proclaimed that 'all men' have the inalienable right to 'life, liberty and the pursuit of happiness.' . . . The author of the Declaration himself, Thomas Jefferson [hoped that the Declaration would be] the signal of arousing men to burst the chains under which monkish ignorance and superstition had persuaded them to bind themselves . . . ."[2] Some, recognizing the presence of humanist tendencies in American thought, feared a pervasive lose of concern for religion and suspected the antireligious undertones of the French Revolution's impact upon American thought to be the culprit. However, most of those living in the newly formed United States were unfamiliar with the issues and ideas, such as French philosophy, that cluttered the minds of the Elite.

Humanism in the United States

Those who sensed a changing "spiritual" landscape, while overly dramatic in presentation, were not far off. Humanist and free thought ideas were present in the United States and were manifest in the ideological stances held by central political figures and the philosophical underpinning of major institutions.[3] For example, even those who did not seek to demolish Christianity, such as Thomas Paine, forced believers to rethink it and defend its doctrine in ways that recognized the Christian Tradition's weaknesses and inconsistencies. And although enlightenment ideas related to free thought, humanism, etc., were under siege during the Great Awakening revivals, this questioning of God and the centrality of humanity was never wiped out. Humanist sentiments continued to grow from this early period and were expressed in far reaching ways through the work of philosophers such as John Dewey and clergy such as former minister of the First Unitarian Church in Minneapolis, John H. Dietrich. In a philosophical and theological turn reminiscent of earlier critiques, the latter argued not for a rejection of religion per se, but for a revamping of the concept by which religion would entail "knowledge of man and our duties toward him." Such a move did not necessitate a denial of God as some feared. But rather it "places faith in man, a knowledge of man, and our duties toward one another first. It is principally a shifting of emphasis in religion from God to man. It makes the prime task of religion not the contemplation of the eternal, the worship of the most high." Energy is given to "the contemplation of the conditions of human life, the reverence for the worth of human life, and the entering into the world that by human effort human life may be improved."[4] For Dietrich, the ethical and moral implications of this position are clear in that the centrality of humanity must mean the preservation and development of "those things which give an ever-deepening value to human life. And so humanism at the very start declares human life to be the things of supreme worth in the universe, insofar as our knowledge goes, and recognizes nothing that commands a higher allegiance." This is not simply an abstraction, a vague moral principle without a practically conceived outcome. To the contrary, Dietrich's humanist vision targets "the pain and suffering, the poverty and misery, the hatred and strife, the ignorance and squalor, and the hundred and one things that afflict humanity and rob it of its right to life and happiness . . . ."[5]

Humans, without the possibility of divine assistance, had no choice but to unite in an effort to develop healthy and beneficial ways of interacting in and with the world. Human values are supreme: "In their effort to offer an affirmation of human worth in the face of cosmic purposelessness, the humanists made man rather than God the creator of values."[6] The ethical and moral implications presented by individual humanists in treaties and sermons were given a more communal and national articulation through the 1933 *Humanist Manifesto*, as well as organizations such as the Ethical Culture Societies and the Unitarian Universalist Association.[7] The Ethical Culture Societies are "dedicated to the ever increasing knowledge and practice and love of the right," and "to assert the supreme importance of the ethical factor in all relations of life—personal, social, national, and international—apart from any theological or metaphysical considerations."[8] The Unitarian Universalist Association is the consequence of a merging of Unitarian churches and Universalist churches during the late twentieth century. The former represented a movement with European roots that insists upon the oneness of God and the humanity of Jesus Christ. It draws from the work of Michael Servetus who proclaimed, during the Reformation, that the Trinity is a misconception. He was put to death for his "heresy," but his ideas continued in locations such as Poland, England, and the United States in the 18th century. Initially, Unitarians were content to espouse their beliefs as members of Congregationalist churches. However, in 1825, they established themselves within their own institutional framework.[9] With time, conflict developed between liberal Unitarian Christians and a segment of the Unitarian movement lead by Dietrich and Curtis W. Reese that called themselves religious humanists. This debate was called the "humanist–theist controversy" and it concluded with an understanding that Unitarians could either be theist or humanist. Unitarianism was carried forth by influential figures such as Theodore Parker and Ralph Waldo Emerson. And, with time members of the Unitarian organization began to move in another direction, giving less attention to the concept of God. In the words of A. Eustace Haydon, "what the gods have been expected to do, and have failed to do through the ages, man must find the courage and intelligence to do for himself. More needful than faith in God is faith that man can give love, justice, and all his beloved moral values embodiment in human relations."[10] Because of natural theological connections between these two organizations centered on the importance of human life, a merger took place in 1961.

The effectiveness of these organizations came with a price. Humanists, particularly those calling themselves "secular," have served as scapegoats. Neoorthodox thought, fundamentalism of various types, the collapse of communism and socialism in parts of the world—all contributed to a radical questioning of humanism's role in the fostering of collective life. Many began to argue that humanism's lack of a recognizable spiritual center or "object" of focused attention would result in its demise, and that traditions with a stronger spiritual base would replace it. Yet, regardless of questions concerning its legitimacy, humanism continued and continues to provide what some consider the best moral and ethical vision of life.

When the makeup of humanist organizations is even briefly probed, a question begs attention: Has humanism only functioned within white communities, or have others embraced it as a viable and vital response to the human condition? African Americans, for one, have embraced humanism—although they have not always used this term—as a dynamic response to social ills faced. But how, when, and why do humanist sensibilities develop in African American communities? In what follows I seek to provide an answer to these questions through attention to the manner in which the humanist principles presented in the introduction to this volume develop within African American life and thought. This is not to suggest that a fully formed system of humanism is present in African American communities from the early years of an African presence in North America. It is more accurate to assert that the nature of life in black America made for fertile ground on which to build humanist sensibilities. But the institutional and more formal structures and patterns necessary as constitutive components of a system were slow in coming and are still in process in African American communities.

Humanism and African Americans: Early Evidence[11]

Slaves were not systematically introduced to the Christian gospel, and radical concern for the salvation of African Americans was not demonstrated until the Great Awakenings which take place some one hundred years after slavery began in North America. Furthermore, the hypocrisy of slave owners and the contradictions between the politicized and economic-driven gospel and the essential sense of self Africans held brought into question the importance of Christian commitment. In the words of an African American spiritual: "Everybody talkin' 'bout heaven ain't goin' there." Suspicion concerning the Christian message was also pointed out by Daniel Payne, in 1839:

> The slaves are sensible of the oppression exercised by their masters' and they see these masters on the Lord's day worshipping in his holy Sanctuary. They hear their masters professing Christianity; they see their masters preaching the gospel; they hear these masters praying in their families, and they know that oppression and slavery are inconsistent with the Christian religion; therefore they scoff at religion itself— mock their masters, and distrust both the goodness and justice of God. Yes, I have known them even to question his existence. I speak not of what others have told me, but of what *I have both seen and heard from the slaves themselves*. . . . A few nights ago between 10 and 11 o'clock a runaway slave came to the house where I live for safety and succor. I asked him if he was a Christian; "no sir," said he, "white men treat us so bad in Mississippi that we can't be Christians." . . . In a word, slavery tramples the laws of the living God under its unhallowed feet— weakens and destroys the influence which those laws are calculated to exert over the mind of man; and constrains the oppressed to blaspheme the name of the Almighty.[12]

It is possible, some might argue, that this slave was in fact a practioner of an African-derived religious tradition. While an interesting suggestion, one I am not in principle opposed to as my work on the importance of "non-Christian" traditions should make clear, it strikes me that there is a fundamental disinterest in theism present, if Payne is to be taken seriously. However, it must be noted that the dominance of Christianity made it difficult for slaves to speak in clear terms concerning an embrace of humanism or, as was often the case, African-derived traditions outside of select areas of North American (e.g., New Orleans). Hence it is possible that this person secretly embraced Voodoo or some other tradition. But it is also possible that the person held to principles that one might associate with humanism as noted in the introduction. Mindful of this, I do not offer this passage as undeniable evidence of a humanist orientation. In providing the above, I am not suggesting that this slave was a humanist. Rather, I am suggesting that an important suspicion concerning basic theistic principles unfolds early in black life. Based upon Payne's depiction, it seems fairly clear that the early rationale for humanism (as opposed to asserting the presence of a fully formed humanism) within African American communities revolved around the inadequacy of Christianity as a response to moral evil. By contrast, humanism, gives more attention to humanity's responsibility for evil in the world, hence humanity's responsibility for reorienting human destiny and fostering equality.

With respect to issues of a humanist cipher of sorts, it is possible that hush arbor meetings and fieldwork arrangements allowed conversation that was humanistic in orientation. Yet, it must be noted that little evidence of this has been recorded, because it would have been considered unimportant by those who thought of the African American life orientation in terms of the Christian faith. Nonetheless, Payne's statement, along with allusions in, for example, some blues tones and African American folk wisdom, point to the presence of humanist principles in early African American communities, but it is not until the African American renaissance (i.e., the "Harlem Renaissance") of the twentieth century that nontheistic orientations are widely presented.[13]

African American Humanism: Twentieth-Century Developments

The beginning of the twentieth century was marked by change. The Great Migration and World War I, for example, brought into question the sense of progress and optimism that marked the prewar period. Even those, however, who questioned war hoped it would end the need for global violence and would result in democratic rule throughout the world. This was the perspective held by African Americans as they volunteered to fight to make the world safe for democracy. Yet as history reluctantly recounts, the war did not change the oppressive nature of U.S. social relations and the inequality of U.S. eco-political interactions. What naturally resulted from continued racial tension at "home" was a disillusionment with the manifest destiny notions that clung to the fabric of U.S. life. The religious rhetoric used to advance sociopolitical and economic goals sounded absurd now, and churches by and large did nothing to correct this. Even black churches, Gayraud Wilmore remarks, failed to provide an adequate response to inequality. What they offered instead involved theological slight of the issue, wrapped in an other-worldly orientation and the rhetoric of spiritual renewal above all else. Those in African American religious studies, due to Wilmore's brilliant analysis, have come to call this ideological shift the "de-radicalization" of the black churches.

Questions of life ignored by otherworldly black churches received more solid attention from some members of the "Harlem Renaissance," who, at some point in life had direct contact with the black church. Their's was a move away from more sanitized treatments of black life, opening the "sacred" or "unspoken" aspects of black culture to critique. For instance, as Arthur Fauset notes, "the church, once a *sine qua non* of institutional life among American Negroes, does not escape the critical inquiry of the newer generations, who implicitly and sometimes very explicitly are requiring definite pragmatic sanctions if they are to be included among church goers, or if indeed they are to give any consideration at all to religious practices and beliefs."[14] Some might argue that because black writers such as James Weldon Johnson explore black Christianity and embrace it as a vibrant mode of cultural expression they must, themselves, accept its basic premises. This logic is faulty. An appreciation for cultural production as such is not an endorsement of the doctrinal assumptions and theological stance of the black church. The following quotation from Johnson's autobiography sums up the overall tone in a great deal of black literature:

> My glance forward reaches no farther than this world. I admit that I throughout my life have lacked religiosity. I do not know if there is a personal God; I do not see how I can know; and I do not see how my knowing can matter. As far as I am able to peer into the inscrutable, I do not see that there is any evidence to refute those scientists and philosophers who hold that the universe is purposeless: that man, instead of being the special care of a Divine Providence, is dependent upon fortuity and his own wits for survival in the midst of blind and insensate forces. . . . All that is clearly revealed is the fate that man must continue to hope and struggle on. To do this, he needs to be able at times to touch God; let the idea of God mean to him whatever it may.[15]

Other literary figures contributed to the advancement of humanist principles with ramifications for daily conduct. Although their writings speak to the larger African American Christian context, this is not a sign of personal commitment. Rather as was certainly the case with James Baldwin, African American Christian expression is understood as an undeniable fixture within African American cultural production but it is also understood as problematic in ways that prevent continuing involvement. He saw in the church an opportunity to develop a "gimmick" that would allow for something resembling life, and he hoped this would also include some comfort from the sense of fault and depravity that pervaded his mind with respect to his sexuality and general life as a second-class citizen, as a "negro." According to Baldwin:

> That summer, in any case, all the fears with which I had grown up, and which were now a part of me and controlled my vision of the world, rose up like a wall between the world and me, and drove me into the church.[16]

Yet in reflecting back, Baldwin recognizes that what drew him to the church was not an urgent concern for the condition of his soul; rather, it was, in fundamental terms a desire for attention and affirmation of his value and "beauty" as a human being. He felt himself needing "to belong" somewhere, to someone. He felt that he could not hold out much longer. And if he must give in, why not the church?

> My friend was about to introduce me when [the pastor] looked at me and smiled and said, "Whose little boy are you?" Now this, unbeliev-ably, was precisely the phrase used by pimps and racketeers on the Avenue when they suggested, both humorous and intensely, that I "hang out" with them. Perhaps part of the terror they had caused me to feel came from the fact that I unquestionably wanted to be *somebody's* little boy. I was so frightened, and at the mercy of so many conundrums, that inevitably, that summer, *someone* would have taken me over; one doesn't, in Harlem, long remain standing on any auction block. It was my good luck—perhaps—that I found myself in the church racket instead of some other. . . . [17]

The question of theodicy surfaced for Baldwin as it does for many who seek to make sense of the world, to find a comfortable and humanizing space in the world, and he attempted to answer it. When all else fails and humanity does not comfort its own, one turns to God. But he discovered, during what the church "folk" called his conversion, in God there was no help. While lying on the church floor, "slain in the spirit," he remarks:

> And if one despairs—as who has not?—of human love, God's love alone is left. But God—and I felt this even then, so long ago, on that tremen-dous floor, unwillingly—is white. And if His love was so great, and if He loved all His children, why were we, the blacks, cast down so far? Why? In spite of all I said thereafter, I found no answer on the floor—not *that* answer, anyway—and I was on the floor all night.[18]

After some years, he came to realize that the Church could not provide the solace he had sought the day he found himself shaking on the church floor. He was " . . . able to see that the principles governing the rites and customs of the churches in which I grew up did not differ from the principles governing the rites and customs of other churches, white. The principles were Blindness, Loneliness, and Terror, the first principle necessarily and actively cultivated in order to deny the two others."[19] He could fool himself and others only for so long, even preaching and the excitement (and acceptance) it brought ultimately could not satisfy his needs and push aside his socio-theological questions. He was still lonely and afraid. Hence, " . . . when I faced a congregation, it began to take all the strength I had not to stammer, not to curse, not to tell them to throw away their Bibles and get off their knees and go home and organize, for example, a rent strike."[20]

Baldwin would preach for three years, but he would ultimately leave the church, and he would find life orientation and meaning in his writing. For him, traditional religion in general and Christianity in particular failed to meet basic needs. Instead, they simply offered a strong push into absurdity, alienation, and race-based demise. Concerning this, Baldwin says, "I said, at last, in answer to some other ricocheted questions, 'left the church twenty years ago and I haven't joined anything since.' . . . 'And what are you now?' Elijah [Muhammad] asked. I was in something of a bind, for I really could not say—could not allow myself to be stampeded into saying that I was a Christian. 'I? Now? Nothing.' This was not enough. 'I'm a writer. I like doing things alone.' . . . 'I don't, anyway,' I said, finally, 'think about it a great deal.'"[21]

James Weldon Johnson spoke of the church and its life because it was familiar and had touched him early. Yet, the cultural production of African Americans and others as chronicled in his *God's Trombones: Seven Negro Sermons in Verse* did not assert an embrace of the supernatural, rather it was a mark of his respect for the work of human hands in altering society. Hence, Johnson's *God's Trombones* is best understood as a defense of African American folk art as opposed to a testimony of personal belief. Although his grandmother, and later his father, attempted to secure his involvement in church, Johnson rebelled. The church, as writings by and about him note, held little appeal:

> As he grew older, James became increasingly discontented with the whole business of religion. He was irked by the constant round of church-going forced upon him by his well-meaning grandmother. . . . When he was nine, James allowed himself to be "saved" at a revival meeting, but, he admitted later, he acted largely out of a desire to please

his grandmother. . . . His doubts concerning religion and the church increased with each year. He could not, however, resolve the tension solely out of his narrow experience with his family or church. It would take a few years, and a sense of life styles beyond the provincialism of Jacksonville, for Johnson to find his answer in agnosticism.[22]

Johnson's agnosticism was most likely enhanced prior to his years at Atlanta University through his work with Dr. Thomas Osmond Summers who embraced science and rejected religion. Through Summers' library, Johnson " . . . found the works of Thomas Paine and Robert G. Ingersoll, America's best known agnostics [perhaps the term humanist is more appropriate]. He read Paine and Ingersoll avidly as nourishment for his earlier vague dislike of conventional religion. By his freshman year, Johnson was one of the two acknowledged agnostics at Atlanta University."[23]

Also of interest for thinking about humanist principles as the basis for praxis is the thought of J. Saunders Redding.[24] Redding recognizes that God and the Christian faith have served a dubious role in the development of the United States. Both social transformation and the oppressive status quo have claimed reliance on God's will. In this capacity, God has both served to humanize and dehumanize. And what is so striking about all of this is the fact that God resides in the collective consciousness as an "implicit assumption." That is, according to Redding, God " . . . is a belief that operates just by being, like a boulder met in the path which must be dealt with before one can proceed on his journey. . . . God is a catalyst, and He is also a formulated doctrine inertly symbolized in the ritual and dogma of churches called Christian."[25] Yet even in light of the manner in which God is woven into the fabric of U.S. life, Redding had his doubts. He notes:

> I do not know how long I have held both God and the Christian religion in some doubt, though it must have been since my teens. . . . I can only think that it came as a result of some very personal communion with God, established perhaps by a random thought, a word, or a certain slant of light through the yellow and rose and purple windows.[26]

Redding combined a growing awareness of whites, and the energetic worship and hysterics of black worship and " . . . realized with deep shame that what the Negroes did on this holy day made a clowns' circus for the whites. The Negroes' God made fools of them. Worship and religiosity were things to be mocked and scorned, for they stamped the Negro as inferior."[27] Redding is not fully aware of the exact progression of thought and insight that led to this final moment, a conclusion that did not shock him nor take him by surprise. It seemed a logical assertion based upon a pragmatic approach to the existential realities of life as an African American. There is an air of comfort accompanying his proclamation:

> I simply rejected religion. I rejected God. Not my instincts, but my deepest feelings revolted compulsively— not because I was I, a sort of neutral human stuff reaching directly to experience, but because I was a Negro.[28]

Yet even with this proclamation the continued appeal to God within his own family and a significant segment of the African American community required an understated rejection, a truce—of sorts—with the notion of God. It is important to note that this truce emerges not because of a personal reversal of opinion, but rather as a means of maintaining a connection with a communal reality beyond himself. Redding writes:

> It was also years before I made a sort of armed truce with religion and with God. I stepped around God determinedly, gingerly, gloating that I was free of Him and that He could not touch me. Indeed, I had to step around Him, for He was always there. He was there, foursquare and solid, at the very center of my father's life. . . . He was in various people I met and felt affection for. He was in the affable, tremulous sweetness of the first love I felt; in the drowning ecstasy of the first sexual experience; in the joy of imaginative creation. But I moved around Him warily, laughing, mocking His pretensions, determined that He would not betray me into Negroness. If there lingered still in the deep recesses of my real self some consciousness of a religious spirit, then the ideal self—the Negro-hating me—did all it could do exorcise [sic] it.[29]

For Redding religion, in this case Christianity, entails the supreme substance of humanity's finer points, and God has been "fashioned" by humans to meet their needs: " . . . God has changed, and though man himself has wrought these changes, he has declared them God's own changes and therefore factors, equations, and of a piece with the mysterious and unknowable nature of God."[30] However, religion has not fulfilled this agenda because it has short-circuited the drive toward social transformation (e.g., race relations) that is the logical end to humanity's better characteristics and sensibilities. That is to say, "religion has become a disembodied sort of activity, when, to be effective, it should be a social function intimately linked up with man's fate on earth."[31] Whereas religion is virtually absent from social issues, God is—unfortunately— present and supportive of the status quo.

The development of humanist principles in the private life and work of African American writers is not limited to Black males. According to Trudier Harris, Alice Walker, and others make use of this orientation in constructing their characters. That is to say, "pattern their [characters'] lives according to values Peter Faulkner recognizes as humanism in its modern sense of an ethic which places human happiness as its central concern and is skeptical about the supernatural and transcendental . . . . The emphasis is on mutual human responsibility . . . ."[32] This position comes across in Walker's work when one considers novels such as *The Color Purple* and *The Third Life of Grange Copeland*. It is also present in her own life and outlook. Noting this, Walker says:

> I seem to have spent all of my life rebelling against the church or other people's interpretations of what religion is—the truth is probably that I don't believe there is a God, although I would like to believe it. Certainly I don't believe there is a God beyond nature. The world is God. Man is God. So is a leaf or a snake . . . .[33]

Alice Walker's humanist principles are deeply contemplative. They entail, in essence, a worshipful appreciation for humanity and for the earth in general. This type of reverence for life gives it godlike status in that "natural life" must remain at the forefront of our thoughts and actions, centering our every move with profound awe. It is reliance on the only force that has demonstrated itself loving: nature. Walker gives flesh to her theological stance:

> I try to imagine my mother and the other women calling on God as they gave birth, and I shudder at the image of Him they must have conjured. He was someone, for all we knew, who actually had said black people were cursed to be drawers of water and hewers of wood. That some people enslaved and abused others was taken for granted by Him.[34]

What is called for, according to Walker, is a recognition of nature as beautiful and beautifully connected to all forms of life. Healthy existence for all is the ultimate concern and proper ethical conduct with respect to nature is the orientation (i.e., environmentalism). Such a system is not a broadened theism; it is "pagan" in part due to the synergy between a celebration of nature and woman. And much of what is necessary for a life well lived is right in front of us. Put differently, "the truth was, we already lived in paradise but were worked too hard by the land-grabbers to enjoy it. This is what my mother, and perhaps the other women knew, and this was one reason why they [women] were not permitted to speak. They might have demanded that the men of the church notice Earth. Which always leads to revolution. In fact, everyone has known this for a very long time."[35] Furthermore, Walker notes, "the 'God' of heaven that my parents and the church were asking me to accept, obscured by the mud, leaves, rot, and bullfrog spoors of this world. How amazing this all is, I thought, entering the muddy creek. And how deeply did I love these who stood around solemnly waiting to see my 'saved' head reappear above the murky water. *This experience of communal love and humble hope for my well-being was my reality of life on this planet.*"[36]

The humanist principles noted in the introduction to this volume and presented in terms of the individual choices of figures such as Alice Walker have been vital for the development of personal identity and social consciousness for many within African American communities. However, the embrace of these principals by individuals acting as such is only part of the black humanist story. One must also take into consideration the involvement of humanists in community and organizations.

The Historical Contours of African American Humanist Principles: Part Two[1]

For some exercising humanist principles, it is useful if not necessary to find a body of believers. That is, the conversion experience—the movement from theism to humanist principles fostered by social and personal issues unresolved by traditional systems—is often furthered by communal interaction. Such a search for relationship is noted in Benjamin May's work on nontheistic perspectives amongst African Americans. Shifting away from theistic perspectives may, Mays remarks, lead some "into the humanistic camp of the Haydon–Otto variety. Negroes would then seek to perfect social change by combining religious idealism and the technique of modern science without relying on God or supernatural aid. The negation of the idea of God may also drive Negroes into the communistic camp, whereby more militant or violent means would be used to achieve political and economic status."[2]

Within the camp of those who sought comfort in the "communistic camp," is the early Langston Hughes. Although I believe he changed his opinion with regard to his embrace of humanist principles as a consequence of the "Red Scare," it is clear that his communist leanings facilitated an independence from the Christian faith as outlined in pieces such as the poem "Goodbye Christ." Although many debate whether Hughes was personally committed to communism, this poem provides a critique of Christianity and a rejection of its theological underpinnings and instead reflects humanist interests held by many African Americans. Granted, there is a tension between this early poem and his later work, but Faith Berry explains it this way:

> ...his attraction to communism has been as misinterpreted as his posture toward Christianity. His reaction to both was to what each

proclaimed: He watched communism hail the classless society, the distribution of wealth, the equality of all, regardless of race or color; he saw Christianity preach the brotherhood of man, alms for the poor, freedom to the oppressed, the kingdom of God. He found Christianity full of broken promises and communism unable to fulfill its promises. Christianity was old. Communism was young. He reached out to both in his youth only to find two Gods that failed. Those who see a dichotomy, a bifurcation, a contradiction, between an early poem such as "Goodbye, Christ" in 1932 as opposed to his more reverent religious works of later years should remember he was always searching for justice for all.[3]

The atheistic stance of the Communist Party and its rhetorical appeal to African Americans (thin as it was) provided a forum and "home" for African American humanists who found churches hopelessly backward and uncomfortable. Documents available at the Schomburg Center for Research in Black Culture (e.g., Universal Negro Improvement Association Papers) and other locations document Party organizing activities in African American communities such as Harlem during the early 1920s and 1930s. Although the Party was reluctant to openly "attack" black church doctrine and practices, some African Americans who joined the Party were more than willing to critique Christian churches. That is not to say all African American communists during this period were humanists or atheists. The work of Robin D. G. Kelley provides contrary evidence when saying "the prophetic Christian tradition, so characteristic of the Afro-American experience, has historically contained a vehement critique of oppression. Ironically, this radical, prophetic tradition of Christianity was a major factor in drawing blacks into the Communist Party and its mass organizations." Furthermore, with respect to particular aspects of the prophetic tradition of Christian faith, Kelley notes that "references" to God and the Bible were not uncommon among Alabama's black radicals. In 1933 the Daily Worker (13 April) received an interesting letter from a black Communist from Tallapoosa County, thanking "God and all the friends of the Negro race that are working for the defense and rights of the Negroes."[4] Nonetheless this support as Kelley points out, was mixed with a critique of less than liberating activity on the part of questionable clergy, who spent their time gaining wealth and preaching against transformation.[5] Some African American communists took this critique further and rejected the Christian church and its doctrine as non-liberating activity and thought. A firsthand account by Hosea Hudson suggests that he, like others, was "rebuked by comments such as "Ain't no God. . . . Nobody ever seen God. How you know it's a God?" When he cited the Bible as his witness, he recalled a common retort, "The white man wrote the Bible."[6] Questioning of belief in the supernatural continued, "I had heard other Party people talking," Hudson says. "Some of them had never been members of no church, talking about there wont no such thing as God": "Where is he at? You say it's a God, where is he at? You can't prove where he's at."[7]

In rejecting God, those using humanist principles Hudson knew in the Communist Party gave humanity responsibility for social transformation. Hudson found it difficult to respond to these charges. In his words:

> I just didn't have a [sic] answer. And them was the kind of questions they put. "If God is such a just God, and here you walking around here, ain't got no food. The only way you can get food is you have to organize. So if you have to organize to demand food, why you going to pray to God about it? Why don't you go on and put your time in organizing and talk to people?"[8]

Although Hudson found these arguments challenging, he recounts that he never lost his belief in God. However, what he states actually sounds like a version of agnosticism. I will not push this point, but instead I will leave it to the readers to decide, based on the following statement by Hudson:

> I never did finally stop believing in God. I haven't stopped believing yet today. I don't argue about it. I don't discuss it, because it's something I can't explain. I don't know whether it's a God, I don't know whether it's not a God. But I know science, if you take science for it, and all these developments, I can't see what God had much to do with it. . . . So it's something beyond my knowledge to deal with. And I don't deal with it. I don't try to deal with it.[9]

By the time African Americans participated in noticeable numbers, the Party had withdrawn from a strong interest in the "negro question" and was concerned primarily with the "Moscow line."[10] While some African Americans undoubtedly remained within the Party hoping for a change, others moved in the direction of black nationalism. Unproductive black churches remained a target of critique during the turbulent years between 1955 and 1970, when the struggle for equality captured popular imagination and political arenas.

The late 1960s witnessed a methodological and epistemological shift within organizations such as the Student Nonviolent Coordinating Committee (SNCC). Gone were its integrationist goals that made it compatible with the Civil Rights Movement; gone was its reliance on

Christian doctrine and paradigms for action. The words found in an early issue of SNCC's newspaper, *Student Voice*, were replaced with determined movement toward self-determination through black power. In 1960, SNCC described its philosophy using the following terms:

> We affirm the philosophical or religious ideal of nonviolence as the foundation of our purpose, the presupposition of our faith, and the manner of our action. . . . Love is the central motif of nonviolence. Love is the force by which God binds man to himself and man to man. Such love goes to the extreme; it remains loving and forgiving even in the midst of hostility. . . . By appealing to conscience and standing on the moral nature of human existence, nonviolence nurtures the atmosphere in which reconciliation and justice become actual possibilities.[11]

It now embraced its own version of black nationalism predicated upon a strong appeal to black power understood in this way. According to Stokley Carmichael and Charles Hamilton:

> [Black power] is a call for Black people in this country to unite, to recognize their heritage, to build a sense of community. It is a call for black people to begin to define their goals, to lead their own organizations and to support those organizations. It is a call to reject the racist institutions and values of this society. The concept . . . rests on a fundamental premise. *Before a group can enter the open society, it must first close ranks.* By this, we mean that group solidarity is necessary before a group can operate effectively from a bargaining position of strength in a pluralistic society.[12]

SNCC decided that social transformation would only occur when African Americans took control of their destiny and worked toward change. Reliance on human potential for empowered praxis was heightened in ways that distinguished this phase of SNCC's personae from the Civil Rights Movement. Although inadequately defined in terms of social transformative thrusts and foci, black power—for some of its advocates—did often allow for rather clearly defined theological assumptions based on humanist principles and articulated using the language of self-determination. This is not to suggest that all members of SNCC (or the Communist Party as discussed earlier) embraced humanist principles. Most certainly did not. However, what I am arguing for is the presence of some civil rights activists who made use of humanist principles as a way of pointing to the praxis-related dimensions of humanism. Take for example, the thought of James Forman, a member of SNCC.

James Forman, in his autobiography *The Making of Black Revolutionaries*, describes his "conversion" to humanism (as defined above) which did not hamper but rather informed his praxis. And his work toward social transformation with SNCC, for example, points to the nature and sustainability of humanist principles as source of praxis. He notes that during his time at Wilson Junior College in Chicago his doubts concerning the existence of God, based primarily on the problem of evil, grew and this process was intensified through contact with questionable Black preachers whose self-centered and selfish ways resulted in his distaste for ministry and the church. Such interactions are summed up by this comment; Forman says: "God was not quite dead in me, but he was dying fast."[13]

After returning from military service some years later, Forman came to a final conclusion concerning the existence of God. He writes that "the next six years of my life were a time of ideas. A time when things were germinating and changing in me. A time of deciding what I would do with my life. It was also a time in which I rid myself, once and for all, of the greatest disorder that cluttered my mind—the belief in God or any type of supreme being."[14] For him humanism required a strong commitment on the part of people to change their present condition, a commitment that belief in God did not allow. That is to say,

> When a people who are poor, suffering with disease and sickness, accept the fact that God has ordained for them to be this way—then they will never do anything about their human condition. *In other words, the belief in a supreme being or God weakens the will of a people to change conditions themselves.* As a Negro who has grown up in the United States, I believe that the belief in God has hurt my people. *We have put off doing something about that because God was going to take care of business in heaven.* . . . My philosophy course had finally satisfied my need for intellectual as well as emotional certainty that God did not exist. I reached the point of rejecting God out of personal experience and observations. . . .[15] (Italics added.)

Critiques of the black church (as a major symbol of theist orientation) based upon materialist approaches to social transformation, for example, continued through the Black Panther Party for Self-Defense. And its commitment to human struggle alone for social transformation houses, from my perspective, theological underpinnings that are humanistic in nature. Reflecting on the ultimate demise of many Black Panthers, Bobby Seales (who, with Huey Newton founded the Black Panther Party) sums up the goals of the Party, goals which echo humanist sensibilities:

> We need activists who cross all ethnic and religious backgrounds and color lines who will establish civil and human rights for all, including the right to an ecologically balanced, pollution-free environment. We

must create a world of decent human relationships where revolutionary humanism is grounded in democratic human rights for every person on earth. Those were the political revolutionary objectives of my old Black Panther Party. They must now belong to the youth of today.[16]

Drawing heavily on Karl Marx, Frantz Fanon, Friedrich Engels, and Mao, the Party initially denounced the church and its teachings labelling both counterproductive. According to Newton, "as far as the church was concerned, the Black Panther Party and other community groups emphasized the political and criticized the spiritual. We said the church is only a ritual, it is irrelevant, and therefore we will have nothing to do with it. We said this in the context of the whole community being involved with the church on one level or another. That is one way of defecting from the community, and that is exactly what we did. Once we stepped outside of the whole thing that the community was involved in and we said, 'You follow our example; your reality is not true and you don't need it.'"[17]

The Party softened its position when it recognized the central role the church held in Black communities. Like the Communist Party, the Panthers' recognized that recruitment would be difficult if open hostility existed with the black churches. Hence, the Panthers fostered a relationship of convenience and socio-political necessity, but without a firm commitment to its theological underpinnings. Newton rationalizes this involvement by arguing a different conception of God, God as the "unknown" that, interestingly enough, science will ultimately resolve. God, then, is not so much a cosmic mystery, but a scientific problem. Consequently, "religion, perhaps is a thing that man needs at this time because scientists cannot answer all of the questions. . . .the unexplained and the unknown *is* God. We know nothing about God, really, and that is why as soon as the scientist develops or points out a new way of controlling a part of the universe, that aspect of the universe is no longer God."[18]

Another voice from the Black Panther Party denouncing traditional black Christian claims concerning the divine was Eldridge Cleaver. Although Cleaver would later give attention to the Mormon Church and Reverend Moon, his thoughts on God and humanity are still worth noting as connected to the desire for self-determination and justice sought by the Black Power Movement. Reflecting on his incarceration in 1954, he writes:

In Soledad state prison, I fell in with a group of young blacks who, like myself, were in vociferous rebellion against what we perceived as a continuation of slavery on a higher plane. . . . While all this was going on, our group was espousing atheism. Unsophisticated and not based on any philosophical rationale, our atheism was pragmatic. I had come to believe that there is no God; if there is, men do not know anything about him. Therefore, all religions were phony. . . . Our atheism was a source of enormous pride to me. Later on, I bolstered our arguments by reading Thomas Paine and his devastating critique of Christianity in particular and organized religion in general.[19]

Echoing the utilitarianism noted above with respect to Newton, Cleaver says: "To me, the language and symbols of religion were nothing but weapons of war. I had no other purpose for them. All the gods are dead except the god of war."[20]

Whether successful or marked by misguided movements, the Black Panther Party's adherence to humanist principles is notable. Attention is taken off of divine assistance; talk of God is ignored. Rather, humans are given sole responsibility for altering the world. In the words of Bobby Seale:

> . . . it is necessary for young people to know that we must use organized and practical techniques. We cannot let ourselves continue to be oppressed on a massive scale. We are not trying to be supermen, because we are not supermen. We are fighting for the preservation of life. We refuse to be brainwashed by comic-book notions that distort the real situation. The only way that the world is ever going to be free is when the youth of this country *moves* with every principle of human respect and with every soft spot we have in our hearts for human life. . . .We know that as a people, we must seize our time. . . . Power to the People! Seize the Time![21]

Explicit Humanist Organizational Force

For those abiding by humanist principles, connectedness to the like-minded can be of tremendous importance because of the typically negative reaction of the larger U.S. society to "nontheistic" orientations. Hence, there are some humanists who maintain a deeply analytical and contemplative stance but as part of a group. For some African Americans the Unitarian Universalist Association has served this purpose, but the UUA's impact has been admittedly small. Its reach has not extended beyond twelve or so integrated congregations. And, according to UUA minister Mark D. Morrison, the African American involvement has not extended beyond roughly one percent of the overall (180,000) membership.[22]

The first attempts to establish the UUA in African American communities centered on the work of former Methodist ministers Egbert Ethelred Brown (Harlem, 1920) and Lewis A. McGee (Chicago, 1947).

After frustration with Unitarians in Jamaica, Brown traveled to Harlem in hopes of fostering the liberal religion message. He devoted a significant amount of time to his ministry, fostering a sense of religiosity connected to a longing for justice and political-social equality, and he drew upon the few socialists, communists, and Garveyites who participated in the Harlem church. Church gatherings usually consisted in thoughtful talks, rebuttals, and discussion; missing was the emotional outburst and otherworldly orientation that marked many churches in this same section of New York City. "While Brown railed at the black churches in Harlem for pursuing otherworldly concerns, he endeavored to make the connection between religion and politics intimate."[23] The format and focus of the church created problems as Brown and its members could not decide on a dialogue platform or a more familiar worship service. Brown's answer was variation:

> He reported that services were modified from year to year, always with the hope of attracting new people. Over the years they varied between a traditional religious service, with hymns, prayers, scripture readings, doxology, sermons, and benediction, and a forum situation, with a strongly secular orientation that included a brief service before the sermons and a discussion afterward. The church's letterhead called the church a temple and a forum. But it was largely upon the forum element that the reputation of the Harlem Unitarian Church was built. It drew people through the quality of its speakers and the open dialogue, yet its character as a forum also left it vulnerable to the kind of disruption described earlier. Moreover, it left some members desiring a service that was more religious in content and format.[24]

Some who desired a more religious, and by this is meant theistic, service complained to Unitarian officials about the atheistic tone of the church. The forum format for services provided a comfortable environment for social activists and others who were interested in opportunities to talk about the conditions faced by African Americans. According to Brown, African Americans needed to be freed from "the emotionalism and superstition and otherworldliness of the old time religion." Furthermore, he understood the Harlem Unitarian church as "a church-forum where the honey-in-heaven and harassment-in-Hades type of religion is not tolerated. There are no 'amen corners' in this church, and no 'sob sister bench.'" Rather, this church called for human action and accountability for the condition of the world.[25] Even with such talk, Brown was Unitarian in terms of christology, soteriology, and concept of God; and the church was marked by the strength of his convictions. Its self-understanding is present in its charter statement:

> This Church is an institution of religion dedicated to the service of humanity. Seeking the truth in freedom, it strives to apply it in love for the cultivation of character, the fostering of fellowship in work and worship, and the establishment of a righteous social order which shall bring abundance of life to man. Knowing not sect, class, nation or race it welcomes each to the service of all.[26]

Until his death in 1956, Brown continued to struggle with this church, while never establishing any significant membership.

In 1947, Lewis A. McGee began the Free Religious Fellowship (initially named the Free Religious Association) in Chicago after having been a part of the Chicago Ethical Society. Starting as a discussion group, the development of this Fellowship stemmed from a lack of attention to liberal religion on Chicago's South Side, an area inhabited by African Americans. The services were conducted as follows:

> The topics presented, in order, were "Why Make a New Approach to Religion," "The Liberal Way in Religion," "Liberalism Faces a Hostile World," "What Is Unitarianism" and "Free, for What?" In each case [McGee] led off with a twenty minute talk and then asked for questions or discussions. These gatherings were marked by a growing interest which became more and more sharply defined toward the possibility of a Unitarian Fellowship.[27]

As with Brown's church in Harlem, some members of McGee's Fellowship were involved with the Communist and Socialist Parties, reenforcing a humanist if not atheist perspective within the Fellowship. This, however, during the years of U.S. communist hunting, caused problems of surveillance for the Fellowship and other Humanist organizations. Most of the members of this Fellowship, unlike Brown's church in Harlem, were African American with some white and Japanese members. While the ethnic and racial makeup was diverse, the reasons for joining the UUA revolved around a common theme. In short, supernaturalism and theological mystery did not address adequately the nature and content of life in the United States.[28]

Many assume that humanist fellowship is limited to cerebral activity with little commitment to more than thought. However, this is inaccurate. McGee's Fellowship, for example, was committed to social action.

In the words of McGee:

> We believe in the human capacity to solve individual and social problems and thus to make progress. We believe in a continuing search for truth and hence that life is an adventurous quest. We believe in the scientific method as valid in ascertaining factual knowledge. We believe in democratic process in our human relations. We believe in ethical conduct. We believe in a dynamic universe, the evolution of life, the oneness of the human family and the unity of life with the material universe. . . . We believe in the creative imagination as a power in promoting the good life.[29]

The Fellowship maintained as its goal the application of its principles within the black community, hoping to attract economically marginal African Americans, even after McGee's retirement the Fellowship continued to function on Chicago's Southside.

Although African Americans have held humanist perspectives and operated accordingly for centuries. The use of the phrase black humanism as a reference is fairly recent. Because the Unitarian Universalist Association was already open to the label of humanism, it makes sense that one of the first, if not the first, references to black humanism would take place within its struggle with race, and advancement of Black power, during the late twentieth century. *Empowerment: One Denomination's Quest for Racial Justice, 1967–1982* provides the following information concerning the use of this term, linking its use with the Black Unitarian Universalist Caucus created to respond to racial issues within the UUA:

> By 1970, the BUUC leadership was beginning to refer to its philosophy of empowerment as "Black Humanism." [A development similar in nature and time to that of Black Theology.] Hayward Henry [former SNCC organizer and member of the board of Second Boston Church] first discussed Black Humanism in the February 1970 newsletter, BUUCVine. . . . Mr. [Benjamin] Scott went on to describe the black interpretation of the [humanist] principles. Black humanists understood humanism as a process, an existential process by which one finds and lives his humanity. To be human is to direct one's own life; therefore, Black Humanism calls for a seizure of decision making and implementation for oneself. Gaining power is an essential element of humanism.[30]

Such a statement allowed for the fundamental elements of religiosity— ultimate concern in the form of human development and ultimate orientation as humanizing empowerment. In addition, this religiosity brought into play the "unique" demands and existential context of African Americans. The value of their "blackness" was brought into human-centered thought and action. So conceived, African American (or black) humanism constitutes an African American religion, a form of religious practice that used (although the relationship was often questioned and dismissed at other times) the UUA to provide institutional structure. Its appeal to social justice is similar to that used historically within African American Christian churches minus one ingredient: justice is demanded and premised upon a "humanocentric" appeal to accountability and progress, and not on the dictates of scripture lived through the Christ figure.

Many of the efforts to express humanist sentiments within the context of community have involved compromise with less welcoming segments of society and intense struggle over the nature of humanist commitment. But what follows is the story of a less "troubled" development.

Norm Allen was born into a Baptist household in Pittsburgh, but one that allowed freethinking based upon only a loose affiliation with the Baptist church. He remembers being allowed to ask questions freely about religion and other topics. And at the age of ten he asked questions about the plurality of religious traditions and which "one" was correct? His mother responded that all we can do is ask questions and follow our convictions. Allen then asked: "what if I reject God?" In response, his mother said that this would be fine if it were based upon his questions and in accordance with his convictions.

His growth into humanism, Allen explains, was based upon his reading of *Free Inquiry Magazine* beginning in 1980, which moved him away from deism and introduced him to the basic principles of humanism (i.e., "human centered approach to life"). The final break with deism came through personal "testing" of the personal deity concept. He began relying on his own capabilities and recognized that the outcome of situations did not differ when he prayed for assistance and when he relied on his own energies and capabilities. He recounts that this break was not a traumatic experience but was a relief. In hindsight, he argues that growing up during the Black Power Movement, he was influenced by the teachings of the Nation of Islam and the Black Panther Party that brought into question the reality and value of Christianity. From this information the "seeds of doubt were planted."[31]

Allen's acquaintance with *Free Inquiry* also sparked his involvement with humanist organizations. From the magazine it was clear that humanism should be concerned with all of humanity, but there was no African American representation. Allen wrote a letter to Paul Kurtz, the editor of *Free Inquiry*, in 1989, voicing his concerns. In July 1989, Kurtz invited Allen to come to Buffalo (New York) and organize a subdivision of the larger organization (Council for Secular Humanism) that would address the questions and concerns of African American humanists. The result was the organization African Americans for Humanism (AAH).

The African American Humanist Declaration presented in 1990 provides useful insights into the nature of the organization and its aims. The writers of this Declaration proclaim that "Today the world needs a critical, rational, and humane approach to living. This is what humanism is all about."[32] Humanism, according to AAH, provides a systematic response to major problems plaguing U.S. society, such as alcohol and substance abuse and economic development issues. It does so by increasing a recognition of human accountability and potential for fostering useful change with attention to certain aims. AAH is committed to a mature and complex community in which individuals are respected and exposed to vital and viable life options as marked by several basic concerns:

- Fight against racism in every form.
- Incorporate an Afrocentric outlook into a broader world perspective.
- Add depth and breadth to the study of history by acknowledging the great contributions made by people of African descent to the world, with the purpose of building self-esteem among African Americans and help-ing to demonstrate the importance of all peoples to the development of world civilization.
- Develop eupraxophy, or "wisdom and good conduct through living" in the African American community by using the scientific and rational methods of inquiry.
- Solve many of the problems that confront African Americans through education and self-reliance, thereby affirming that autonomy and free-dom of choice are basic human rights.
- Develop self-help groups and engage in any humane and rational activity designed to develop the African American community.
- Emphasize the central importance of education at all levels, including humanistic moral education, developing a humanistic outlook, and pro-viding the tools for the development of critical reason, self-improvement, and career training.[33]

The presence of humanist principles within African American communities has a long and complex history, with respect to both indi-vidual perspective and communal understandings and actions. Recognizing this history and connecting it to the larger reality of African American cultural memory will go a long way in clarifying and appreciating the various ways in which African Americans have struggled for and celebrated a richness of life.

Section II

Examples of Humanist Principles as Life Orientation

I have no doubt that the avowal of my liberal opinions will drive many from me who were once my friends and even exclude me from many platforms upon which I was a welcome speaker, but such is the penalty which every man must suffer who admits a new truth into his mind. I am sensitive to the good opinions of men and shall suffer-but I am in a measure prepared for whatever may come to me in this respect. As to my not going far enough, I have to say, that while I am free to follow my convictions wherever they may lead-I deem it wise to avow those which are perfectly formed, clearly defined, and about which I am entirely undisturbed by doubts of any sorts. I bow to no priests either of faith or of unfaith. I claim as against all sorts of people, simply perfect freedom of thought.

—Frederick Douglass

It is one thing to espouse humanist principles as theoretical framework, and it is another to live out these principles. Moving humanist princi-ples from abstraction to life practice involves a certain stance regard-ing life circumstances. How, for example, might the black humanist appeal to her life principles regarding recent social developments and political debates fostered in part through a surge in fundamentalists attitudes and demands? In this situation, how might humanist principles define an appropriate system of social ethics? How might the humanist respond to such challenges through a structured life that promotes health and justice in light of the antibody culture promoted by fundamentalism? In such a situation, humanist principles promote a measured optimism with respect to human potential for just living. Yet this does not promote nihilism in that humans are also perceived as being creative and motivated creatures who are capable of positive movement in the world. We, according to humanism, stand alone as fully accountable and responsible for the bettering of the world. And our success with respect to this task is not measured in terms of final outcomes, but instead is measured in terms of praxis. There is a sense of urgency regarding this work in that, unlike fundamentalists, humanists argue that a good life here is the best we can hope for.

African American Humanist Principles as Ethical Framework: The Religious Right and Doing "Right"[1]

Many argue that humanist principles are faulty because they lack both a moral center and the accompanying system of ethics necessary for productive living in this world. I argue that humanism as defined by the principles presented in the introduction to this volume, because of its agenda and concerns, is premised on an undeniable system of ethics and a moral code capable of moving human society in positive ways. This seems perfectly clear to me, but not to others. For example, why do fundamentalists—in the form of the New Religious/Political Right (NRPR)—fail to see this?[2] The answer to this question, I believe is found in the very fabric of fundamentalist assertions.

I am not interested in providing a detailed history of this phenomenon, I will make a few quick statements related to fundamentalism's historical development. In this way I hope to rehearse some objections of fundamentalists to humanism and, in turn, offer a humanist response. My goal here is not to suggest that fundamentalists should be (or even could be) conversation partners for humanists. If presenting conversation partners were the focus of this section of this book, I would turn to liberal theologians and others who more clearly share a critique of fundamentalism and misguided Christianity. I give attention to fundamentalism here because of the consistency of its attack on humanism and the manner in which humanist response serves to illuminate the nature and meaning of the humanist principles presented earlier.

Although some argue that a fundamentalist ethos surfaces through the conservative evangelical leanings of many pre-twentieth century preachers, we will focus on the development of fundamentalism in the early twentieth century as a response to the socialized gospel, based on a rationalized faith and the downplaying of personal salvation.[3] Rationalized is the operative term here in that it points to fundamentalism's preoccupation with modernism.

Although fundamentalists were concerned with growing liberal trends in theology, their major objection to modernism revolved around evolutionism and the manner in which this called into question basic scriptural "Truths." This challenge, combined with the changing nature of U.S. society as a global "Power" based upon World War I, shook what many conservative Christians considered the firm foundation for life in the United States. In other words, the postwar years presented new challenges that held the potential to destroy the world through a profound faithlessness. In more recent years, fundamentalists have noted the manner in which late-twentieth-century liberalism, marketed through civil rights and civil liberties organizations and movements, threatens the basic structure of life in the United States. For the NRPR, the sickness spread by these organizations and movements is exemplified by restrictions on prayer in schools, legalized abortion, the trivialization of creationism, etc.[4]

Fundamentalism in the form of organizations such as the Moral Majority (1979) does not respond to these threats with sackcloth and ashes, and detached spirituality. To the contrary, the New Religious/Political Right makes use of religious rhetoric and doctrine for very mundane purposes. In spite of an initial marginal status and periods of decline, fundamentalism has grown through various activities that link doctrine (re-enforced through Bob Jones University, Liberty Baptist, the "700 Club," and other outfits) with efforts to bring both private and public existence in line with biblical principles. The various branches of the New Religious/Political Right have, over the past several decades, grounded social, political, and economic concerns in a strong appeal to scripture and Christian principles.

Fundamentalism affirms two basic points: (1) an absolute and divine authority over all areas of life recognized through doctrine and, (2) a system of ethics publicly acknowledged and enforced by the state.[5] This two-prong theo-democracy of sorts is premised upon three central workings. The first is a revisionist history that highlights the past greatness of the United States as undeniably grounded in obedience to God's various laws. In this manner, the NRPR seeks to reimagine the United States along the lines of those who took and then physically (as well as intellectually) carved up

North America. It is a throw back to manifest destiny arguments and the U.S. "chosen status" complex these arguments entail. Second, theo-democracy demands a clear dichotomy: rewards for those who obey God and punishment for those who disobey God. Premised on this is a forceful call for ethics and morally centered activity based on the New Testament call for faith *and* works. Finally, there is a need for identifiable sources of good and evil; the latter having a direct relationship to non-Christian religions and organizations perceived as antireligion.[6]

It should be noted that not all conservative Protestant leaders and their groups consider themselves part of the NRPR. According to Samuel S. Hill and Dennis E. Owen, Billy Graham, Wheaton College, Calvin College, Fuller Theological Seminary, and the Southern Baptist Convention, for example, disclaim any connection with this move-ment.[7] Yet, questions raised by other conservative Christians have not significantly hindered the agenda and activities of the New Religious/ Political Right. The NRPR dismisses criticism through the assumption that critics fail to adequately embrace Christian principles. In short, from the perspective of the New Religious/Political Right, those who embrace the gospel of Christ and the values it teaches must be in line with the NRPR.

Having some sense of what fundamentalism, in the form of the New Religious/Political Right, affirms as well as its basic ideological framework is there any wonder why humanism finds itself under attack? According to Stephen Johnson and Joseph Tamney:

> Just as there are "positive symbols" for New Right ideals, there are "negative symbols" for what the New Right considers evils. Foremost among these negative symbols is *secular humanism.* . . . Secular human-ists, as portrayed by prominent New Right leaders such as Jerry Falwell . . . reject or ignore the existence of God, have raised human beings above God, and encourage "moral relativism and amorality, [that] challenges every principle on which America was founded." Simply put, secular humanists are anti-God, anti-family, and anti-American. . . . The New Right belief system goes further, and posits secular humanism as the ruling ideology of the state, especially the educational system. Therefore it must be fought.[8]

While denying the charges brought against humanism, I do acknowl-edge, as chapters one and two demonstrated, that there is sufficient reason to believe that humanism has had a long history within the United States. In fact, basic humanist principles have helped to guide this country's development with respect to positive values and aspirations. Fundamentalists, of course, deny humanism this type of positive contribution to ethics and morality.

What Fundamentalism Doesn't Say

Humanists can never hope, nor should this be their goal, to convince fundamentalists of humanism's moral center; the fundamentalist's perspective relies too heavily upon "revealed" materials and a faith stance that are by nature only partially open to reason. Rather, humanism should seek to clarify for itself the ethical stance and moral center it assumes, and in the process point to its transformative potential to those who might be open to dialogue. That is to say, humanists should concentrate on living out their principles.

Corliss Lamont, who has written classic treatments such as *Humanism as Philosophy*, argues that humanism as a system is defined by eight basic propositions. They can be summarized as follows. Humanism rejects notions of the supernatural, and recognizes Nature as the basis of all life. Attached to this is an understanding of humanity as an intimate component of nature that developed through a process of evolution, not creation, and with death human personality ceases to exist. Connected to this linking of body and mind is an understanding of reason or thinking as the result of humanity's interaction with the natural environment. Hence, ideas cannot be separated from experience. Through reason and the advances of science, humanists believe humankind is capable of solving its problems; in this sense humans are, in the words of the poet William Ernest Henley, masters of their own fate.[9] Lamont asserts that humanism entails an appreciation for culture and works to advance the arts. This includes respect for nature that requires efforts to safeguard it. Connected to this is concern for humanity across the globe demonstrated through efforts to ensure peace and health. Finally, these principles, according to Lamont, are enacted through an ethic that "grounds all human values in this—worldly happiness, freedom and progress—economic, cultural and ethical—of all mankind, irrespective of nation, race or religion."[10]

The connotations of these principles fosters a balance between individualism and a concern for community. That is to say, humanists, based upon the above principles, are responsible for living in the world in ways that promote both individual happiness and the welfare of the larger community.[11] Ultimate happiness is only achieved, therefore, through service to others.

The principles outlined by Lamont, including the vague sketch of a humanistic ethic, predate the publication of his book. In fact, in 1933, a group of humanists—clergy, academics, and others—felt the need to clarify exactly what humanists think and do. This took the form of the *Humanist Manifesto I*.[12] Drawing from ideals noted in the founding documents of the United States, humanists such as philosopher John Dewey, clergyman John H. Dietrich, and 32 others presented the basic humanist perspective. In the words of the 34 humanists who signed this document:

> The time has come for widespread recognition of the radical changes in religious beliefs throughout the modern world. The time is past for mere revision of traditional attitudes. Science and economic change have disrupted the old beliefs. Religions the world over are under the necessity of coming to terms with new conditions created by a vastly increased knowledge and experience. In every field of human activity, the vital movement is now in the direction of a candid and explicit humanism.[13]

As those who have studied this document often indicate, it stands upon three secure pillars: reason, science, and democracy. Attached to these three pillars are the following ideas: (1) Humans are part of nature and nature reflects an evolutionary process, not a moment of divine creation; (2) a rejection of a mind/body split based upon a sense of reason and experience as codependent; (3) Supernatural rationales and explanations for human life are rejected, and religion is understood as being a human construct; (4) human potentiality and creativity must be exalted and both personal fulfillment and social well-being promoted.

Manifesto I quickly became dated because of new world concerns and problems such as World War II and the Civil Rights Movement. As a result, it was necessary to update the manifesto in light of new and pressing concerns. This new document, *Humanist Manifesto II* (1973), expanded the issues addressed in the 1933 manifesto, and also presented a more developed and more mature system of ethics grounded in human experience and situational in that it was open to change as the needs and problems of the world changed.[14] In part, this situational ethics was a response to Christian notions of ethics that anchored what humans "ought to do" in often unyielding divine revelations and mandates. In opposition to this, *Humanist Manifesto II* called for an ethical system of conduct that called attention to "united actions—positive principles relevant to the present human condition. [It is] designed for a secular society on a planetary scale."[15] Ethical conduct requires a respect and appreciation for the insights of groups other than one's own. All of this is balanced by "compassion, empathy", and tolerance. There is a sense in which this optimism, according to *Manifesto II*, must be tempered and contained. By this I mean it must recognize the horrific deeds done by humans toward other humans and the larger reality of Nature. Understanding this, humanism asserts liberation or transformation as a possibility but in no way guaranteed.

Adhering to these precepts, humanists seek to enhance freedom and dignity—individual fulfillment and communal health on all levels of existence—within an open, peaceful, and global society. This is not a penultimate development, but to the contrary "what more daring a goal for humankind than for each person to become, in ideal as well as practice, a citizen of a world community. It is a classical vision; we can now give it new vitality. Humanism thus interpreted is a moral force that has time on its side. We believe that humankind has the potential intelligence, good will, and cooperative skill to implement this commitment in the decades ahead."[16]

It does not take much insight to recognize the optimism implicit in the above pronouncement. Is there really any other way to read such a proclamation—"Humanism thus interpreted is a moral force that has time on its side"—without taking away the intended tone and texture? Even attempts to temper the strength of the humanist's embrace of progress allows the assumed power of human ingenuity to bleed through. Philosopher Paul Kurtz provides an apt example when raising an unavoidable question: "If all moral systems are products of human culture and if we remove the self-deceptive faith systems that sanctify them, is it still possible to lead an authentic ethical life in which a responsible morality can be developed?"[17] While quite a challenging question, Kurtz does not hesitate to answer with an emphatic yes. His basic assertion affirms the individual's ability to maintain an ethically and morally sound life without a theistic orientation. Humanism does not, of necessity, collapse into a state of nihilism. In fact, the radical sense of accountability and responsibility humanism requires of humanity can foster a strong sense of creativity and ingenuity leading to self and social transformation.[18]

How does one act upon this conviction? First, humanists assert that humans have an obligation to value time and to bring fullness to each moment because we only have this one physical existence. Furthermore, humans must work toward individual development, and the construction of a larger society in which all have healthy life options and positive avenues for fulfillment based upon full human rights and civil liberties. Also indispensable to this process is a recognition of humanity as a part of Nature without special status and without the possibility of appeal to a "higher power" capable of breaking into and altering history. (It is no wonder that so many humanists are actively involved with organizations such as the American Civil Liberties Union—ACLU.)

This system of ethics recognizes the risk involved in living, and acknowledges that our success with respect to the above striving will be accompanied by moments of failure. Yet, this does not result in despair and apathy because the system of ethics embraced by humanists entails a repostulation of what it is to achieve and be successful. What becomes important is not the "end" of struggle—guaranteed outcomes—rather, success is located in positive action itself. Fundamentalists, as you can imagine, find this troubling because it does not recognize a teleologically defined sense of history imposed by a divine presence. In short, for the fundamentalist "all things are possible" because God is able to break into human history and transform it, with humans as foot soldiers, so to speak. Humanistically defined ethics negates this theological assumption, and brings into question the narrowly conceived sense of democracy espoused by many NRPR groups. The humanist system of ethics has the potential to point out the dangerously xenophobic nature of the NRPR's democratic vision. Fundamentalists maintain a rather narrow reading of the Bible, ignoring the undertones and challenges to the status quo promoted by Christian scripture. Therefore, their notion of democracy is also narrow because it seeks to maintain bad political and social policies we should have abandoned long ago. These policies destroy from within—dehumanizing all involved.

Humanism points to fundamentalism's roots in a profound sense of dread and despair that limits social transformation by forcefully pointing to what humans are incapable of doing or being without a divine "restraining order." Humanism offers an alternative that recognizes both the promise and pitfalls of human existence and seeks to guard against the dangerous reification of opinions and behavior, while also guarding against a romanticizing of the human animal. Jean-Paul Sartre's words concerning existential humanism (humanity as sole "law maker" as opposed to the human as an end/higher value) help illuminate the point I wish to make. "If one calls every attitude of unbelief despair," Sartre remarks, "like the Christians, then the word is not being used in its original sense. Existentialism isn't so atheistic that it wears itself out showing that God doesn't exist. Rather, it declares that even if God did exist, that would change nothing. . . . Not that we believe that

God exists, but we think that the problem of His existence is not the issue. In this sense existentialism is optimistic, a doctrine of action, and it is plain dishonesty for Christians to make no distinction between their own despair and ours and then to call us despairing."[19]

Ultimately the best response to the fundamentalist challenge is to live out of a commitment to human life and a healthy world, giving full recognition to the various hues of this commitment. It is through active commitment to life—in all its diversity and complexity—that humanists point out the flawed democratic vision espoused by the New Religious Right and offer another way. Humanist ethics and principles of life are centered on a simple *modus operatum*: live in ways that enliven and further develop oneself and the larger community.

The Christian Right and Soteriology: A Humanist Alternative[1]

I suggest we begin by recognizing that enthusiasm for religiously based solutions to sociopolitical dilemmas facing the United States is not a recent development. It's historical roots run much deeper than that. Over the course of the nation's life, from the Great Awakenings of the 1700s and 1800s to the present, segments of the aggressively religious have interpreted their historical situation by means of a theology of disconnect. That is to say, they viewed the problems faced by the United States, problems that threatened, from their perspective, the viability of the nation, as stemming from a failure to maintain commitment to the teachings of Christ. Let us take the period of the Civil War as an example. Concern with the spiritual condition of the United States dominated the thought of many Methodists. Some of the more aggressive holders of this mindset took it upon themselves to spark a holiness campaign to enliven a national devotion to God, thereby recapturing the revival fervor felt early in the nation's life. This push toward greater religious commitment and devotion was made in the south as well as the north. In places like New Jersey, camp meetings began to take place, giving shape to a more general call for holiness, recorded in the New Testament, and articulated through a discourse of spiritual authority tied to historical transformation. The reach of holiness and other evangelical perspectives was rather broad if one keeps in mind, for example, that the Democratic party ran William Jennings Bryan, an evangelical, as its candidate for the presidency in 1896.[2]

One can make a reasonable argument for thinking about a fundamentalist ethos surfacing through the conservative evangelical leanings of many nineteenth-century Americans, an ethos that continued into the early twentieth century. As noted in the previous chapter, fundamentalists opposed any challenge to biblical authority and tradition.[3] Mindful of this, the twentieth century, according to fundamentalists, presented new challenges that held the potential to destroy the world through a profound faithlessness—marked by evolutionism, Marxism, and so on.

Until the middle of the twentieth century, fundamentalists in different forms fought the growing secular sensibilities of American society. Religion remained important during this period, yet American religious culture was dominated not by its more radical and fundamentalist dimensions, but by those segments that were more comfortable with an increasingly secular society.[4] The socio-political and cultural turmoil of the late 1960s—including the civil rights struggle opposed by many fundamentalists, the Vietnam War, and a general feeling of cultural relativism—sparked a resurgence of radical evangelical principles based on an old idea: The United States suffers the possibility of collapse because of a moral relativity and denial of fundamental religious principles. Only a return to the guidance of God for *all* life decisions can change this path of destruction. In more recent years, fundamentalists have noted the manner in which late-twentieth-century liberalism, marketed through civil rights and civil liberties organizations and movements, threatens the basic style of life in the United States. For the Christian Right, the sickness spread by these organizations and movements is exemplified by restrictions on prayer in schools, legalized abortion, the trivialization of creationism, etc.[5]

During the 1970s a rather aggressive mode of fundamentalism surfaced with an eye on reshaping the United States' moral consciousness and sensitivity to the will of God through political and social intervention. TV evangelist Jerry Falwell spoke to this engagement in 1976 when saying: "This idea of 'religion and politics don't mix' was invented by the devil to keep Christians from running their own country."[6] What we uncover here is a reactionary and theologically based nostalgia—a desire to re-create American life along the lines of a restrictive and biblical model. Referring to the 1980s, Jerry Falwell claimed "there has never been in our history, in modern history, a time when a nation, the great nation of America, that God could make a spiritual turnaround such as is occurring in this country. America is in the midst of spiritual renaissance."[7]

In spite of an initial marginal status and periods of decline, this brand of evangelicalism has grown through various activities that link doctrine with efforts to bring both private and public existence in line with Christian sensibilities—grounding social, political, and economic concerns in a strong appeal to scripture.

The goal of the Christian Right was to bring the United States under the authority of scripture, adjusting its moral and ethical compass in accordance with Christian principles and assumptions. Put differently, Christian Right activism and thought sought, according to Walter Capps, "to bring religious beliefs and political ideals into mutually sustaining alignment, to stabilize the vitality of the nation's common life."[8]

It is difficult, and scholars agree on this, to access the success of the Christian Right with respect to its political agenda. For instance, it has made some gains with respect to "access to public facilities for private activity," as well as some concerns that both Christian Right supporters and detractors could agree on such as the 1979 legislation in North Carolina that prevented regulation of private schools by stating that "in matters of education . . . No human authority shall, in any case whatever, control or interfere with the rights of conscience."[9] Yet, its fight against humanism has not been as successful. For instance, a suit against the Alabama State Board of Education revolving around a creationism versus humanism debate did not produce the sought after restrictions of classroom information to creationist accounts of humanity.[10] Furthermore, the Christian Right's fight against homosexuality and pro-choice policies has also failed to bear the desired fruit because it has been unable to impose its myopic vision of conduct on the larger society. Even when courts place restrictions on conduct such as the requirement "that minors notify their parents before having abortions . . . these restrictions have been upheld for nonreligious reasons . . ." Overall the Christian Right's record is mixed at best and does not demonstrate signs of mounting strength and influence.[11]

Moving from legislation to political office, the Christian Right's track record is not much better. Accordingly, "one can find hardly anyone since 1980 claiming major electoral victories for the NCR [New Christian Right]. Not even NCR spokesmen or conservative sympathizers have often made such claims, which come most frequently from anti-NCR organizations such as People for the American Way . . . . Where NCR organizations and their critics appear to agree is that the NCR has shifted its attention from important large constituency elections (Congressional or gubernatorial, for example) to small constituency elections that are severally unimportant (school boards, for example)."[12] Although somewhat successful, particularly outside the national political scene (keep in mind the decline of the Moral Majority and its inability to force the fulfillment of its agenda for the Republican party after the 1980 election), mass mailing, television spots, and other modes of access to the homes and minds of Americans have not resulted in a forceful shift in the orientation of U.S. life. But could we actually anticipate more than moments of success on minor issues when the Christian Right is not the result of an evangelical consensus, but rather required the support of other conservative groups often with differing motivations and constituencies?[13]

The Christian Right's strength certainly wained after 1984, although it maintained throughout the late 1980s consistent support from roughly 15 percent of the white population.[14] Attention was turned in the 1990s to grassroots activism through organizations such as Pat Robertson's "Christian Coalition." Because the Coalition is ecumenical overagainst the religious narrowness of other Christian Right organizations, it achieved a broader support base. Nonetheless, Robertson's miserable showing in his quest for high office, and his inability to really affect Republican politics, resulted in his return to his television program, "The 700 Club."

While the relatively contained impact of the Christian Right is an interesting story to tell, and certainly provides a sense of relief for the humanists in our country, what I find most intriguing about the Christian Right is not its record of political success but rather the theological preoccupations that give raise to its socioeconomic and political sensibilities and activities. And I like to frame these theological preoccupations in terms of soteriology or in simpler terms, issues of salvation. This is not to suggest that members of the Christian Right think only in terms of heaven or go through the course of life thinking only about the second coming of Christ; there is a concern with what Walter Capps refers to as "the spiritual vitality of the nation," a God-based strength that sustains the country through its presence or diminishes the country through its absence.[15]

The Christian Right's rationale for personal spiritual development and public activism stem from a common root sensibility—a recognition of a profound tension between this world and the spiritual realm of God that must be ultimately resolved through divine action and human work. Furthermore, this resolution has ramifications with respect to the individual's soul and the soul of the country. If we are not careful, the argument goes, humanism and liberal Christianity will destroy both souls through human arrogance's denial of divine authority, a morally repugnant secularization of life. With each passing day the urgent nature of reform and realignment with the will of God grows because we are close to the apocalypse. As Jerry Falwell, a major figure in the Christian Right during the 1980s, warns, "undoubtedly we are at the edge of eternity."[16]

A Focus on Salvation and Christ's Return

Developments in the United States were and remain, according to the Christian Right, deeply connected to the current dispensation. We must recognize, however, that some fundamentalists did not embrace dispensation formulations. And, for other fundamentalists dispensational thought made political engagement futile: Why participate in the sociopolitical dimensions of a condemned world? For others, practical activism was not the proper response to the dispensational millennialism impulse because the condition of the United States merely pointed to the return of Christ and the development of a new order. The ideas of divine punishment and divine reward are the underlying rationale for much of what is said and done by the Christian Right. Whether one talks in terms of early evangelical activities marked by the holiness movement or more recent fundamentalist activities exemplified by the Christian Right and its leadership, there is an underlying principle that informs the critique of liberal theology and changing societal vision, values, and mores. This principle means of measure is defined by the requirements outlined in scripture concerning preparation for the return of Christ. One might refer to such a stance as being sensitive to apocalyptic possibilities and salvation history because "Christians through their actions today cannot alter God's plan, but they may be enacting it. Their actions may prefigure or typify the events of the Second Coming of the Lord. Thus, born-again Christians, through the lens of Bible prophecy, read history backwards. Future events, which are fixed and known, determine—if only in the sense of enabling Christians to imagine—the shape, the content, and the significance of present events and actions."[17] While more forceful and explicit millennialism is rare, there remains a concern with the fulfillment of God's will, the completion of history.

Rather than focusing on the destruction of a wicked world as the climax of history, the more prominent members of the Christian Right speak in terms of America's "special" role in history. This exalted status assures the ranking of the United States as "the center for a great spiritual and moral reform that will lead to a golden age or 'millennium' of Christian civilization."[18] Implied by this depiction of the USA is a theological adjustment to the typical discussion of the rapture and the tribulations that mark the return of Christ and would most likely also mark the demise of the United States. As part of this re-envisioning, preachers from various places on the Christian Right spectrum argued for a period of refinement by which "the period before the rapture, the end-time, was now understood to be a time in which God would judge Christians, as opposed to Jews. And his judgement was not fixed by biblical prophecies. It was, in other words, reversible. If Christians responded to God's call through holy living and moral action, God would spare them and the American nation. Thus, with this little tribulation, Bible prophecy teachers opened a small window of progressive history in the last days, a brief moment in time when Christians could, and must be, agents of political and social change."[19]

Even this public face of evangelical thought is supplemented with a continuing concern for relationship with God. Hence, moral reform can save the Nation and personal commitment to Christ can save the individual. This is why Hal Lindsey—author of the 1970s best-seller *The Late Great Planet Earth*—said ". . . we must actively take on the responsibility of being a citizen and a member of God's family."[20] One can add to this, Jerry Falwell's 1984 insight:

> On the Christian campuses all over America kids are not only winning souls and loving the Bible and loving Christ, they're becoming good citizens. They are getting registered to vote; they are getting informed. They are determining that we are no longer going to lose by default . . . We're going to do something, we're going to have revival, and we're going to have restoration, and the rebuilding of this great nation, so that out of a society and an environment of freedom we might evangelize the world in our generation, and before the rapture, take a multitude on to heaven with us.[21]

If Lindsey and Falwell are correct, the United States becomes a proper station for the climax of history with the coming of Christ, and the saved individual gains a place in this new order, a glorious existence in God's Kingdom.

Even for those who are less interested in direct attention to the second coming of Christ, there remains in place a view of the world that is preoccupied with reward and punishment. Such a framework requires a profound commitment to God and God's teachings as the only way to secure the proper life path, and the successful movement through this troubled world. While engagement within the world is mandatory—"in the world but not of it" is the typical mantra—it is undertaken through a perception of important bible-based knowledge and a final outcome that is not completely measurable through mundane shifts in society. Ultimately it is a question of salvation framed by a concern with the end of human history as we know it; and the final phase of the Christian Right's work entails preparing individuals and the nation for a glorious role in the unfolding of God's cosmic blueprint.

It is interesting to note that in a sense the Christian Right's agenda is concerned fundamentally with conversion: individual surrender to and movement toward God and God's will, and a reversal of the country's slide into secularization and moral decay as a form of collective salvation. As one member of the Christian Right remarked: "We must work to better the world because the Bible tells us to, and we must await Christ's return because the Scripture commands us to do so."[22] In both instances, the preoccupation is with salvation and the redemption of history—the divide between heaven and hell and those who struggle to obtain the former.[23]

Salvation and the Afterlife?

Salvation is an interesting theological and, to some extent, political category. And, attention to the nature and meaning of salvation and heaven might shed useful light on the preoccupations of fundamentalists and evangelicals in general and the Christian Right in particular. Recognizing the connections between current forms of evangelical and fundamentalist thought and their early influences in the colonies and England, let us begin with a story, one of Christian, a man seeking righteousness and a proper relationship with God. The teller of Christian's story, puritan preacher, John Bunyan (1628–1688), says:

> So I saw in my dream that the man began to run. Now he had not run far from his own door, but his wife and children perceiving it began to cry after him to return: but the man put his fingers in his ears, and ran on crying, "Life, life, eternal life." So he looked not behind him, but fled towards the middle of the plain.[24]

These lines appear very early in John Bunyan's account of the journey from sin to salvation. Bunyan, a minister who faced imprisonment because of his religious beliefs, uses this metaphorical account (written at least in part during his second imprisonment) to explain his and every Christian's struggles with the flesh and the demanding life that will ultimately lead to salvation—eternal life in the afterlife. The quotation marks the anxiety and dread experienced by the text's protagonist—Christian—upon realizing his state of condemnation and the requirement for redemption from the city of destruction.

He, with the help of the "Evangelist," realizes that he must run the path that will lead to the Celestial City—Heaven. It is only after many trials and tribulations, first the forsaking of his family, Christian moves from the weakness of the flesh to life eternal.[25] According to Bunyan, every Christian must encounter sinful moments, strong temptations, self-doubt, *suffering*. All of this should be dealt with gladly, if not embraced, because it is the manner in which salvation is won and heaven gained. Such profound effort is rewarded by an afterlife. "No cross, no crown," as some church folk say.

Bunyan's is not an isolated mode of religious thought. In fact, by the time Bunyan embraces this theological position, it is well worn. Let us take St. Augustine[26] as our pre-Bunyan example of this argument and then, through a huge historical leap, move toward the late twentieth century. St. Augustine argues that "original sin" resulted in a distortion of the image of God housed in the human frame. Because of this mutation, humanity is prone to sin and "by the time of Augustine, the Church had settled down in Roman Society. The Christian's worst enemies could no longer be placed outside him: they were inside, his sins and his doubts; and the climax of a man's life [was] . . . conversion from the perils of his own past."[27] Of course the wages of sin are death—eternal damnation, removal from the presence of God for the endless days of eternity. Only with God's grace and gut wrenching human effort can this proclivity be overcome and humanity restored to right relationship with God, culminating in life after death in the glow of God's glory.

In the beginning, for Augustine and other Christians, God created humanity to praise and worship God—to be with God. The fall of humanity prevented this connection to God. Salvation entails this recognition and a commitment to purifying oneself to carry out this purpose. And the afterlife, housed in heaven provides an endless devotion to God, an endless Sabbath. In the words of St. Augustine:

> The sixth [day] is the one in which we now are. It is an age not to be measured by any precise number of generations, since we are told: "It is not for you to know the times or dates which the Father has fixed by his own authority. After this 'day,' God will rest on the 'seventh day,' in the sense that God will make us, who are to be this seventh day, rest in Him . . . . Suffice it to say that this 'seventh day' will be our Sabbath . . . . On that day we shall rest and see, see and love, love and praise—for this is to be the end without the end of all our living, that Kingdom without end, the real goal of our present life."[28]

St. Augustine argues for an understanding of heaven and the afterlife as the proper outcome of a life well lived. For those who do not embrace God and God's call to righteousness, the afterlife entails eternal torment in the pit of Hell. Readers will notice the scriptural basis for this: "The wages of sin are death, but the gift of God is eternal life."[29]

Many Christians argued for proper conduct as a means by which to gain the favor of God and eternal life. Even when Christians did not understand heaven as a physical space or a concrete and existential reality, it served as a powerful metaphor denoting the desired presence of God in a community of believers living in peace and prosperity. Underlying this was a desire for spiritual and physical freedom from the harshness of mundane existence; and the philosophical underpinning of this desire is a notion of "progress" and the assumed teleological nature of history. Despite current circumstances, the religious person often looked toward heaven and the afterlife, and felt confident that the "world" ultimately makes sense. It makes sense because this life is followed by one of total happiness and fulfillment.

The affirmation of an afterlife results from two related if not dialectical issues: human arrogance and human hardship. Based on a rather problematic reading of the first testament (i.e., the Hebrew Bible, the Book of Genesis), many have assumed humanity is God's finest creation, the master of the world. In giving the first human control over the naming of the remaining creation, many assume that God gave humanity control over the rest of earth's life forms—to "name" is in many ways to "own." In addition, the command to "have dominion over the rest of creation" assumes a radical degree of control that has fostered harmful anthropomorphism. Human ways of being in the world are considered supreme; being at the "top" of the food chain has profound consequences. Then, of course, God is more concerned with human life than with any other form of created existence. Such a wonderful life form must certainly have significance beyond this mundane world.

Maintaining this view is not as easy as it may appear because of the interruption we know as death. We, humans, are conscious of our dealings and dread the end we know must come. Death is a part of life, and we must live mindful of this. To leave behind what we have come to treasure is angst—existential terror. Humans crave resolutions to complexity; we seek to lessen the tension caused by paradox. The uncertainty of "reality" beyond the grave is such a complexity; we cannot scientifically test it for confirmability and so we seek to resolve it in other ways. The possibility of nothingness—a permanent end and detachment from what we cherish—is too imposing, too "final" for many. Heaven and life lived there do for many religious communities what scientific and naturalistic rationales cannot. Some project life beyond this for comfort, comfort that "superior" beings undoubtedly deserve.

The careful reader will detect the sarcasm and existential leanings couched in the above discussion. However, there is truth in my statement. The perception of humanity as, on the whole, exceptional and more closely connected to the divine than any other creature easily lends itself in the religious mind—particularly within the Christian Right—to hopes for eternal life—the afterlife. Does not God want God's best creation around forever? Is not each individual who recognizes this and correctly worships God entitled to live "forever"? Yet, even this metaphorical use—this revisionist language—often conjures up a world in which intolerance and exclusion are still practiced. Think of this, who is excluded from "heaven"? The excluded are often synonymous with those labeled social misfits by the Christian Right: In the antebellum years native Americans and blacks, more recently the list has expanded to include homosexuals and so on.

Humanists such as Richard Wright brought to our attention something that we already knew but were reluctant to own: Life seems absurd and meaningless. Those things we cherish only bring temporary fulfillment, and more commonly collapse under the weight of oppression, mistrust, greed—angst. This can produce feelings of resentment, loneliness, alienation, isolation—nihilism.[30] Although there are countless examples of those feelings emerging during the ebb and flow of U.S. history, the experience of African Americans in the U.S. context has raised them in paradigmatic ways for all who call this land home. Floyd Hayes has it right:

> for African Americans, racial domination is both a historical and a contemporary phenomenon. One can trace its genealogy back to the period of the Atlantic slave trade and chattel slavery when slave traders and slave-owners sought to dehumanize captured Africans. Herein lies the original cause of the long nightmare of African-American resentment. Slave traders and slave-owners based the entire filthy enterprise of chattel slavery on the premise that black people were subhuman property, to be used, but not respected. As Orlando Patterson has written, enslavement constituted for captured Africans a form of "social death".[31]

From the postmodern perspective, everything is decentered, and the certainties of the modern age are understood as illusionary. Everything is open to questioning (deconstruction); nothing is certain. Take for example the words of Richard Wright, who, when speaking about the nature of southern life as contextual reality and metaphor for U.S. race relations, points to the heart of this absurdity:

> The next day when I was already in full flight—aboard a northward bound train—I could not have accounted, if it had been demanded of me, for all the varied forces that were making me reject the culture that had molded and shaped me. I was leaving without a qualm, without a single backward glance. The face of the South that I had known was hostile and forbidding, and yet out of all the conflicts and the curses, the blows and the anger, the tension and the terror, I had somehow gotten the idea that life could be different, could be lived in a fuller and richer manner.[32]

Life is cruel and unforgiving; to some extent I must agree with the Christian Right on this. To think otherwise is to render suspect the tenets of humanism I hold dear. Yet, there is a spark of hope, the "idea that life could be different;" an impossible possibility that the world will not only survive but transform itself even in the midst of human generated turmoil. Humanists such as Wright temper this hope, this possibility. Wright is a humanist who understands that if the world changes, if humanity is "redeemed" it will be the result of human activity and agency, a dangerous proposition at best. And this transformed existence ends for each human life through the completion of life's cycle in death. There is nothing beyond death for us. Nonetheless, somehow, this can be enough. The possibility of making this life meaningful and connected is enough.

Humanism's naturalistic response to the question of human life beyond this world does not satisfy most. There is too much left open, too much comfort with paradox and uncertainty. When faced with human disillusionment, alienation, misconduct, oppression—the abhorrent "stuff" of human existence—many look for comfort beyond the chaos.[33] When confronted by unsettling realities, Christians have often resorted to a heavenly gaze and a preoccupation with the afterlife—using proper conduct on earth as a training ground of sorts. Thoughts of the afterlife—a time of perfect living free of this world's problems and preoccupations—dominate discourse and underlay the rationale for "worldly" activities undertaken by the Christian Right. This preoccupation with salvation in transhistorical terms actually stymies efforts to transform society, to increase healthy life options. Whether the result of human arrogance or human fear, the "afterlife" preoccupation is in large part due to a misconception of the "life well lived." Such thoughts have taken away from the push to transform the world by our hands; the "afterlife" allows humans to look beyond this transformative activity with a clear conscience. These ideas do not promote sustained efforts to liberate life *on* earth. They, in fact, provide an escape hatch from the seemingly overwhelming problems of human life. In a very real way, talk of salvation and the afterlife, as found within the framework of the Christian Right, is a human construction that stifles the living of life with appreciation for its thickness and unpredictableness.

Section III

Instances of Humanist Principles as Hermeneutic of Human Integrity

While listening to the vivid language of the sermons I was pulled toward emotional belief, but as soon as I went out of the church and saw the bright sunshine and felt the throbbing life of the people in the streets I knew that none of it was true and that nothing would happen.

—Richard Wright

As for me, I do not pretend to read God's mind. If He has a plan of the universe worked out to the smallest detail, it would be folly for me to presume to get down on my knees and attempt to revise it. That, to me, seems the highest form of sacrilege. So I do not pray. I accept the means at my disposal for working out my destiny. It seems to me that I have been given a mind and will-power for that very purpose.

—Zora Neale Hurston

How does one make sense of the world, interpret its developments, inspect its positive aspects, and address its warts? This section seeks to address this question by giving attention to social developments ripe for analysis. The concern is with the placement of black bodies in public spaces, and the existential and epistemological ramifications of these bodies in various social locations. Rap music, once thought a fad, is a major cultural force that gives expression to the angst and interests of young people in their most graphic forms. Often presented as predators, the young black men who dominant this art form have gained the attention of local and national figures over the years, and they have come to inhabit the fears of these figures, who express in social policies and political moves a concern with the chaos it is assumed these rappers represent (whether their music critiques or celebrates "gangsta" life is of limited concern where the status quo is concerned). In the popular imagination of the United States, these young male bodies have come to symbolize a problem that must be confronted and controlled. And this attitude is not limited to the representatives of hip hop culture. Black bodies in general are seen as dangerous. One gets a sense of this desire to control or "fix" certain bodies through the practice of racial profiling, and the "sex-ing" of black bodies. Several questions must be addressed: Is there anything of humanist value in rap music? What is the appropriate humanist approach to racial profiling? And, how might humanists discuss the issues of sex and sexuality inadequately addressed by religious institutions and society in more general terms?

Humanist Principles, Musical Production, and Life Orientation[1]

Most, whether articulated in this way or not, are troubled by a general disregard for life. Many will note this with respect to the numerous individuals hurt if not killed during the process of car jacking, for example. This "jacking" is far from a simple desire for material acquisition without delay; it involves an epistemological decay, a devaluation of life and a general sense of hopelessness and meaninglessness. Human life and the products humans create have equal value for "small-time criminals" and white-collar criminals who hide behind large desks in corporate offices. Unfortunately, we have had to become somewhat numb to this reality—attempting to recognize it and act accordingly without being consumed by it. The need to make sense of the world and not be overwhelmed by absurdity has required this. But we have not considered this ideal and we assumed that effort and commitment could result in a better way—movement away from the absurdity and madness of contemporary life. Many have looked to religious organizations and institutions for this. The phenomenon of the "mega-churches" speaks to the appeal of religious answers to pressing problems. And why shouldn't this be the case? Religious answers and spiritually inspired action have often worked in the past: Keep in mind the Civil Rights Movement. Yet, this movement toward the churches and other religious organizations seems somewhat matched by a disregard for the sanctum of houses of religion. That is to say, unspeakable acts—racism, sexism, homophobia, greed, and so forth—within the religious sphere have gained attention; and for many, have reduced religious organizations' ability to claim exemption from the fallout resulting from social conditions. Hence, they are treated no differently than other buildings and corporations. One should not assume that religious organizations have just begun to exhibit the flaws and shortsightedness that mark other human realms; it just seems that this is the last place where most of us want to be confronted by the shortcomings we know all too well.

Religion, as human enterprise, is not free of human flaws and idiosyncrasies. This much must be granted. However, religion—flaws in tow—allows us to think of ourselves while still thinking of something much greater than the individual. Whether this is called "God" or by another name is unimportant. What is important is the way in which religion can create a sense of balance—a recognition of the individual as part of a much larger reality and, by this recognition, make advances toward a valuing of life above products. This is what religion, at its best, is about—the development of healthy life options, the ability to creatively imagine new possibilities and new potential. And, in this way, religion—in general terms—helps us to maintain our "cool-ness," while acting in accountable and responsible ways to improve a world that seems "jacked."

There is a link, a rather strong and persistent link, between religion as a response to the absurdity and terrors of life and cultural production such as music. What I mean by this is in part captured in Gerald H. Hinkle's summary of Nietzsche on art: "when the will is most imperiled, art approaches, as a redeeming and healing enchantress; she alone may transform these horrible reflections of the terror and absurdity of existence into representations with which many may live."[2] Or, as Michael Gardiner argues in his discussion of Bakhtin and the metaphorics of perception:

> we are literally "thrown" into an external world of brute facticity, consisting of objects and events that confront us and demand some sort of response. In reacting to this pure "giveness", each of us is animated by a dynamic impulse to "sculpt" or transform the discrete elements of this object-world into coherent and meaningful wholes, and we are forced to make certain choices and value-judgements with respect to our Being in-the-world. We are compelled to produce meaning in a world lacking intrinsic value, to transform this proffered "giveness" into meaningfulness.[3]

In other words, the arts—or cultural production in more general terms— are shaped by a concern with "thick" issues having ontological and existential weight. Unpacking the signs presented by various cultural artists can shed light on the human quest for additional meaning, for a greater sense of place and space. As Paul Tillich phrased it decades ago, "pictures, poems, and music" are significant with respect to the study of religion in that they express "some aspects of that which concerns us ultimately, in and through their aesthetic form."[4] There is something of significance in the artistic tension between form and content. Visual arts, decorative arts, music and so on say something of importance concerning the creative and imaginative ways in which we forge meaning, the manner in which rap artists for instance provide an assessment of life carved out of metaphors, signs, and symbols.

I am not suggesting that every form of cultural production undertakes this process with the same level of intentionality and intensity, nor with the same level of accomplishment and long lasting value. To make this claim would entail denying those in the study of religion (and other disciplines) the ability to adequately critique cultural production, and I want to maintain the viability of "criticism and the question of artistic excellence."[5] Both interpretation of the art form and the intent of the artist are conditioned by historical realities and concerns, and say something about the human attempt to make sense of our past and present in ways that speak to the future in urgent and moving ways.

The Contours of Black Humanist Principles

There is, I believe, an underexplored mode of religious engagement that has captured the imagination of some for whom dominant religious faiths such as the Christian Church and Islam prove unhelpful. Many of those frustrated by these modes of orientation have embraced humanism. During the course of the following pages, I unpack certain genres of rap music for the manner in which they embrace and articulate the basic principles of humanism.[6] In order to accomplish this, several points are explored. I begin with a brief explication of humanism as a mode of religious orientation.[7] Finally, I give attention to various artists and their music as examples of humanism's development within the world of rap music.

I must admit that denial or downplaying of humanism's presence in various communities has subsided in my professional circles, and outside these circles its principles are embraced by various groups and recognized as guiding their relationships and perceptions of life. However, what remains a battle ground is the proper way to categorize humanism: is it a religion? A philosophy? Unlike many inside and outside humanist camps, I argue that humanism *can* be understood as a mode of religious expression, or of life orientation.

Academics and nonacademics alike, are too quick to think about religion and define religion in terms of traditional, institutional forms. While institutions, doctrines, and rituals are important, religion should not be reduced to these things. Religion in fact has a more elemental nature that gives raise to institutions and doctrine, but is not limited to them. And it is this elemental nature that links what might appear to be opposed modes of orientation. The rituals and doctrines, institutions and practices represent only the historical manifestations of a more basic impulse. Religion's basic structure embedded in history, is a general quest for complex subjectivity in the face of the terror and dread associated with life within a historical context marked by dehumanization, objectification, abuse, intolerance, and captured most forcefully in the symbol of the "ghetto." What results from this tension and dread is a sense of loss, of one's being slowly disappearing, or as rapper ScarFace remarks, "I know I'm here somewhere, but I can't find me." This is, it seems according to ScarFace, the natural consequence of the world's absurdity, a place in which there are "too many motherfucking questions, and not enough answers."[8] Religion's purpose involves a recovery from this absurdity, and the finding of one's full value and meaning.

This quest for complex subjectivity means a desired movement from life as corporeal object, controlled by oppressive and essentializing forces to a complex conveyer of cultural meaning, with a detailed and creative identity. This subjectivity is understood as complex in that it seeks to hold in tension many possibilities of being, a way of existing in numerous spaces of identification. It seeks to hold together all of these various threads of identity development in a way that makes them essential components of a larger, tangled, and all encompassing sense of being in more absolute terms. In this sense, it is the struggle to obtain meaning through a process of "becoming". "To become human and develop a human identity," philosopher Robert Birt says, "is a process of invention (self-invention), of personal and collective action conditioned by social relations. . . . Thus, oppression may be seen as an existential violation, an ontological crime. Is this not what is meant when we describe oppression and exploitation as dehumanizing? But since this violation of the human being is social, the struggle to create an identity is also social."[9] Birt speaks of consciousness and social realities in ways that shadow my understanding of religion. What I see as the inner impulse and its manifestations are similar to what Birt describes as consciousness and social realities as dependent realities. That is why, according to Birt, " . . . there can be no social liberation without a liberating consciousness."[10]

Point of Clarification: Humanity/ Humanitarianism—Not Humanism

I want to make a distinction at this point between humanizing rap music and humanist rap music. The former entails attention to the full development of human potential, but it is discussed and promoted in ways that do not necessarily bring into question principles and assumptions that run contrary to the humanist sensibilities outlined in this book. A clear example of humanizing rap is found in the lyrics of KRS-One (*Knowledge Reigns Supreme Over Nearly Everyone*). KRS-One (born Lawrence Parker) became a major figure in hip hop culture through his socially and politically conscious rap done in collaboration with Boogie Down Productions. Recognizing his interest in theological and philosophical concerns often ignored by rappers, several commentators have labeled KRS-One's collaborative work and his solo projects in particular humanistic in nature. Mark LeVine, for example, in an internet article titled "KRS-ONE: Hip-hop Clergy" categorizes his rap style as "a philosophically and even religiously 'humanist' perspective in hip hop."[11] The approach noted by LeVine often involves a questioning of religious doctrine and institutions such as those one finds in his critique of Eurocentric readings of scripture in "Why Is That?" What KRS-One offers, is a human-centered mode of theistic orientation, what William R. Jones might label "humanocentric theism."[12] This approach entails a tension between divinity and humanity whereby the accountability shouldered by humans for the development of human fulfillment is highlighted but within the context of a world housing the divine.

The above reflects the take on human history presented in one of KRS-One's more recent projects titled "Spiritual Minded." In "Take it to God," KRS-One provides an embodied theology, but this theology does not mean, in vulgar terms, the pronouncement of the "human as the measure of all things." God seems transpersonal, transhistorical, and the final source of meaning. Why else would listeners be told to "run to God, and let him in your heart?"[13] However, it is possible to read this song and much of what one finds on the CD as metaphorical, as an appeal to human ingenuity, a push for listeners to find themselves and increase their consciousness as the ultimate act of meaning; and in the process they become god-like. There is an ambiguity in KRS-One's philosophical stance that does lend itself to this type of interpretation, particularly when one considers his construction of hip hop as a "new" religion, complete with the understanding that rappers are god-like because of their ability to create through the word. In their raps, language takes on a type of materiality—a creative process similar to what the first several chapters of the Book of Genesis seek to portray. Turning again to the internet, where much of the conversation concerning rap takes place, this perspective on rappers is alluded to by a commentator who says: "the storyteller assumes the role of evangelist, and the rap becomes a chronicle of the messiah. These songs are at one and the same time 'about the rapper' and 'by the rapper,' in the same way that the Bible is both 'about God' and the 'Word of God' simultaneously."[14]

KRS-One understands the performance of rap as a "sacred" act, one growing out of and extending to the audience his commitment to the best of the Christian faith. In other words: "We go into the clubs with these kinds of message [sic], going straight to people who didn't come to the club to hear nothing about Jesus, nothing about Christ, nothing about God, nothing about the Bible, not about nothing—they came to party. What we do with that audience, right there and then, is you know what, before you leave here today consider your relationship with Jesus Christ . . . We're under the impression God don't need no help because God is infinite, all-seeing, all-knowing, all-loving, a graceful, merciful God. But the truth of the matter is the great omnipotent God Almighty needs our help."[15]

KRS-One's is not necessarily a faith tied to institutional forms, but one that is more in line with a general sense of spirituality or connectedness to the divine that is hampered by most institutions. KRS-One spoke to this perspective during a recent interview: "From day one we came in with a deeper level of consciousness and discussed God and Christianity on each and every album. But most people when they look from a critical eye, they don't believe you could be a Christian and question the Bible or the Church. They think being a Christian means keeping your mouth shut, be quiet or apathetic in the face of injustice and blatant lies. I don't think Jesus intended that for any of us."[16] This spiritual consciousness does not equate to humanism as defined in this book. In fact, it runs contrary to the non-supernatural sensibilities that inform humanism. Perhaps it is better to describe KRS-One's project as radical humanitarianism, based on a fundamental appreciation for humankind, as opposed to humanism.

There is something important in Queen Latifah's work, from a humanist perspective, that also warrants consideration. Queen Latifah's celebration of the body speaks to notions of complex subjectivity that are compatible with humanism on the existential and social levels. Through her appeal to the importance and beauty of the body, she links her music to the blues presented by figures such as Bessie Smith, Ma Rainey, and Koko Taylor who fought against dehumanization— the terror of an over-determined identity—through a bold embrace of black flesh. Taking up this issue, particularly with respect to women, she remarks in her inspirational book published in 1999: "Find power. Find the queen who lives inside of you, embrace her, nourish her, praise her, hold her accountable, and love her. Become her."[17] For Queen Latifah, the development of self-consciousness, the type that promotes a determination to make the most of our opportunities and to demand respect based on a recognition of our human worth, is vital. One certainly gets a sense of this perspective in early hits such as "Ladies First," that serves to epistemologically link Queen Latifah to legends like KoKo Taylor, whose "I'm a Woman" demanded a "space" for women in music and the larger world. The former's rap is the work of a queen of rap, or "princess of the posse," the latter is the proclamation of the "Queen of the Blues." Queen Latifah speaks of the glory of black womanhood in words that sparkle with confidence. Her success is a clear example, she argues, of the general success black women are capable of achieving, and to miss it one "must be blind" to miss seeing a black woman "standing up on her own."[18] Koko Taylor placed a similar emphasis on the ability of music to speak to the human situation and provide motivation for improvement, as she noted during an interview: "My music is healin', you know? It's healin', it's therapy, it's encouragement."[19]

There is a tradition within black music of appreciation for black bodies, a loving of black bodies "fiercely," to borrow a word from Toni Morrison. One can trace this thread in numerous ways and through various genealogies and genres, including the link between the blues and rap stated above. Yet, Queen Latifah's appreciation for black humanity, the importance of sensory experience, also shares a "rhythm" and sensibility notable in the work of humanist author, Alice Walker. The humanism informed paradigm of "womanist" behavior outlined by Walker in the early 1980s jibs with the "nature of a sista" presented by Queen Latifah almost two decades ago. Within the definition of "womanist," Walker speaks of the creativity and ingenuity, the determination and steadfastness, by which black women have celebrated their bodies and spirits. There is, it is abundantly evident in Walker's work, a 'power to . . .' that bubbles out of healthy self-consciousness—a sense of self in connection to a mighty past full of important, creative, insightful, and strong people. And part of our task is to recognize the invaluable links between the past and the present, the manner in which what we are and will become is dependent on the work of those who have come before, involving a synergy by which the world has a richness, but not "simply rich because from day to day our lives are touched with new possibilities, but because the past is studded with sisters who, in their time, shone like gold. They give us hope, they have proved the splendor of our past, which should free us to lay just claim to the fullness of the future."[20] This appreciation for the ancestors—within the context of race, class, and gender—encouraged in works such as *In Search of Our Mothers' Gardens*,[21] finds its way into rap music through Queen Latifah. Evidence of this appreciation is expressed by Latifah in prose as she reflects on her mother: "in many ways, she was the queen who gave me the guts and the confidence to become one myself. She gave birth, physically and spiritually, to Queen Latifah."[22] There is undeniable beauty and worth housed in the physical frame. Bodies, according to Queen Latifah, have an importance not simply because of the spirit lodged within them. They have an importance, or invaluable meaning, in and of themselves, and this importance is not reducible to the utility of various body parts. No objectification. And for those who try to diminish her humanity, Queen Latifah makes known that she brings "wrath to those who disrespect me like a dame."[23]

Walker's hermeneutic of womanist reflection also promotes an appreciation for the human body, but there is a different epistemological basis for her stance in contrast to that of Queen Latifah. A connection between humanity and the rest of creation is existentially and ontologically endemic to Walker's conception of human life. It is this connection that we must nurture and celebrate. In a very real sense, nature (and the universe) can be understood as God: "God is everything that is, ever was or ever will be."[24] Yet, for Walker, this does not promote a typical theism—recognition of and allegiance to a supernaturalism hitched to a transhistorical and transpersonal reality, a cosmic personality guiding the universe from a distance. Rather, her perspective is better described as a modality of humanism by which humans act in accordance with "a belief in their own judgement and faith in themselves."[25]

Queen Latifah's honoring of the black female's spirit and body is tied to a reverence for the Christian God as the source of humanity's authority and meaning. She raps about the "divinity" of the black woman, but this sense of divinity seems measured in terms of intrinsic beauty and worth, and does not challenge the sovereignty of God and the general merits of supernaturalism.[26] The rapper is not seeking a Nietzchean removal of God from the throne and the subsequent increase in human potential. In fact, this divine being, God, is the prerequisite for self understanding because "everything starts with God. . . . If I don't believe in God," Queen Latifah states, "I can't have faith in anybody else, including myself. If I can keep my connection to God—keep my faith—I can conquer everything."[27] Walker finds traditional theism's historical connection to dehumanization too thick, too deep, too troubling. Instead, she moves toward nature worship, recognizing the Earth is God, "and Nature as its spirit."[28] For Latifah, the connection between humanity and God is positive and exemplified by her relationship with her mother, the person who introduced her to theism. For Walker, the story is different. In her words:

> It is ironic, to say the least, that the very woman out of whose body I came, whose pillowy arms still held me, willingly indoctrinated me away from herself and the earth, from which both of us received sustenance, and toward a frightful, jealous, cruel, murderous 'God' of another race and tribe of people, and expected me to forget the very breasts that had fed me and that I still leaned against. But such is the power of centuries-old indoctrination.[29]

Both Queen Latifah and Alice Walker recognize the harshness of this world, and the particularly strong bias against black women, and both push for a recognition of the beauty and creativity of black women. For Walker traditional modes of theism such as Christianity and the church serve only to hamper the formation of healthy humans. But for Latifah, relationship to the Christian God is the elemental source of beauty and human fulfillment. Both would agree on the importance of reclaiming black bodies but only for Walker is this in essence a humanist act.

Rap and Humanist Principles: Rejecting Traditional Religion

One can think about humanist sensibilities as being expressed through the effort of some rap artists to reclaim the black body (as biochemical and physiological reality) within the context of history and culture. And so, for example, while the group Arrested Development advocates earth-based and African-derived modalities of spiritual development in much of their music, there is also a critique of institutional modes of religious experience.[30] What one gets is an empirical method of exploring the nature and meaning of life in that some rap artists, like Arrested Development, check the validity of traditional claims regarding the human condition against the norm of liberation. A clear example of this movement is found in track 8, "Fishin' 4 Religion" on Arrested Development's debut CD, *3 Years, 5 months and 2 days in the Life of* . . . Shifting his gaze to black Baptist churches, Speech, Arrested Development's leader, proclaims that his move outside the church is premised upon the church's flawed theology which does not allow for social transformation. Instead it offers an overly spiritual-ized depiction of life that pacifies the oppressed as it encourages them to praise "a god that watches you weep but doesn't want you to do a damn thing about it."[31] The alteration of this theological pit involves: "Baptist teachings dying [as] the only solution."[32] There is a sense in "Fishin' 4 Religion" that fulfillment of human potential must be designed and plotted within the realm of human interaction and experience. Soteriological considerations are earth bound.

An appeal to a humanist ethic of the mundane, is even more tellingly played out in ScarFace's "Mind Playin' Tricks 94." An extension of the track recorded by the Ghetto-Boys, ScarFace acknowledges the existential angst resulting from a life of conflict and urban struggle. He entertains the nihilism and self-destruction often associated with a godless existence, and he expresses the internal dilemma in ways reminiscent of Richard Wright's existential leanings: "dear dairy, I'm having a little problem with my mind state. How many bullets would it take to change my mind quick? Sometimes I want to end it but I don't though."[33] He is encouraged, the story goes, to talk with his pastor, but to no avail because the church is marked by radical individ-ualism and a gospel of greed by which ministers are guilty of "putting a price tag on the man's word . . . . and they opening up these churches for some quick cash."[34] There are theological and ethical shortcom-ings marking the church that only amplify the hardships and deadly "hustle" that. define life as ScarFace knows it. His solution, to the extent it can be considered one, is to reject institutional religion and engage a humanist ethic of self-help by giving "money to the most needy and never put it in the hands of the most greedy."[35] One can raise questions concerning the strength of this ethic as it is preached by a character whose life is marked by self-generated trauma. What is of importance, however, is the advocation of this humanist ethic, a movement beyond a theistically oriented ethic. ScarFace would not be the first to suggest a model of conduct that he does not personally live out. The practice of the humanist perspective is flawed in much of rap music, yet this is not an indictment of the humanist principles themselves.

Moving from Critique toward New Sensibilities

Tupac Shakur's attention to humanity's ethical ambiguity, as I interpret his lyrics, as well as his preoccupation with human accountability for transformation move rap beyond humanism as critique or deconstruction. While some might disagree with my interpretation, arguing for a more Christian-based orientation for Tupac, I believe what follows offers more than a plausible depiction of his work. Take, for example, "Blasphemy," found on *The Don Killuminati*. The ethical and moral outlook presented in "Blashemy" as thug life is bleak, marred by breakdown of communal relationships and structures, and premised upon a somewhat warped individualism as the guiding principle of survival. An anthropology of human original sin as some type of cosmic stain is not the source of this predicament. Humanity is prone to much destruction simply because "niggas gon' hate for whatever you do." In other words, ethical and moral shortcomings just are. But there is a tension between this depiction of human nature and a recognition of the ability of human's to act in more productive ways because, as Tupac notes, "ain't nothing free, give back what you earn."[36]

No doubt, there are legitimate questions one can raise concerning the significance of this proclamation within the given context of "thug" life. Yet, it seems Tupac attempts to respond, in subtle and metaphorical tones, through an embodied theology by which the nature of life as a thug is reimagined. For example, on the track "Hail Mary," Tupac provides an alternate christology, one in which the Christ figure and his energy are represented in the context of "thug" turmoil as the authentic ground of transformation.

There is an almost surreal quality of redemption brought through the presence of the thug, exemplified by Tupac and his THUG LIFE (*The Hate U Give Lil Infants Fucks Everybody*).[37] The reality of the thug and thug life present an opportunity to restore order. While it might not include sensibilities we are comfortable with, and I certainly do not promote or justify the destructive elements of this ethic, it provides a necessary function. There is a significance given to the thug by Tupac that might be explored in terms of Rene Girard's work on violence and the sacred. One could also think in terms of Albert Camus' Cain, or Richard Wright's Cross Damon.[38] In all these cases, the existentialism of Camus or Wright and the philosophy of order presented by Girard, there is a constructive dimension to the scapegoating of "misfits" as the horrific and dangerous carrier of social dis-ease, and sacrificing them for the maintenance of a more 'orderly' system of relationships. Tupac recognizes this sacrilizing and sacrificing of the scapegoat in "Hail Mary."

The line between innocence and guilt and the meaning of this distinction is blurred, but one finds in "Hail Mary" a sacrifice of some for the benefit of others. Is not this one way to explain the image of "brothas" being crucified graphically articulated by Tupac? Tupac seems to see it this way: "tell me I ain't God's son." This linkage to sacrifice and its ramifications is the underlying premise of his embodied theology and its radical reformulation of the Christ event. Tupac draws on the New Testament's basic rationale of the presence of God in human flesh; but this time, alluding to himself, the purpose is to "lead the wild into the ways of the *man*" (hauntingly reminiscent of something Richard Wright's Cross Damon might speak), and the ultimate location of this work is not transhistorical in any sense, but in flesh.[39] While this is clearly a step toward Camus' critique of the Christ event, its hermeneutic sensibilities provide a blurred resemblance to the existential suspicion of Christianity and the human alternative.[40] Tupac's 'blasphemy' against traditional modes of religious expression—his radical humanizing of christology—seeks to break the illusion of life provided by religious theism. To this end one might think about Tupac as a rather loose version of what Camus labels the "rebel," complete with the existential and ontological questions and commitments that mark and litter the rebel's environment which is, according to Camus, "a society where a theoretical equality conceals great factual inequalities."[41] There is an uneasy possibility for life marked by this attitude, one that is firmly lodged on earth, in sensory experience:

> If we decide to rebel, it must be because we have decided that a human society has some positive value [in this case a "thug" society]. But in each case the values are not "given"—that is the illusionist trick played by religion or by philosophy. They have to be deduced from the conditions of living, and are to be accepted along with the suffering entailed by the limits of the possible. Social values are rules of conduct implicit in a tragic fate; and they offer a hope of creation.[42]

Tupac inverts or humanizes the story of the Christ event in ways that locate a parallel significance in human interaction. Tupac rebels, through a 'thugafication' or blasphemy, against metaphysical responses to life. In his illusions to this event, there is no real appeal to transhistorical realities or transpersonal modes of historical intervention. The laws by which Tupac lives in "Blasphemy" are not from Christian scripture but are humanity-derived lessons. Historical developments appear the only reality worth addressing in any substantive way, with thug life as an emblem of true struggle as "the media be crucifying brothas severely. Tell me I ain't God's son."

Tupac offers the ultimate humanizing of theology, complete with a theodical twist—a theological and religious mode of musical heterodoxy—understood in terms of human existence: "is god just another cop waiting to beat my ass . . . ?"[43] What does one do in face of the universe's silence concerning our predicament? According to Tupac "God promised, she's just taking her time." Responses to such questions are not to be found in traditional religions because religious leaders and scripture do not address the realities of life in a "thug nation." To the contrary, through metaphor, signs, and symbols, Tupac suggests the response to life's ultimate concern is found in an epistemological and existential shift away from religious traditions.

While Tupac makes rhetorical use of the "God" concept, the final answer to the absurdity of life is in human activity. At best God is suspect because in a thuged-out Marxist twist, there is a link between deception and the presence of traditional religion. For example, traditional religion is metaphorically identified with the drug trade in that it is "God's words all crushed like crack." There is, then, little hope for social transformation to be found in theistic religion for those who search for "truth" in that "truth" is "where it's hard to find God."[44] In opposition to traditional modes of religion, Tupac offers another tradition, a new system of thought and practice, perhaps forged during his "exile" or imprisonment. It is, he argues, centered around "the saint for thugs and gangstas—not killers and rapists, but thugs. When I say thugs, I mean niggas who don't have anything."[45] The traditional, transcendent God is replaced in everyday dealings with the Black Jesus, who Tupac believes operates through—not against—the community of thugs. "I feel like Black Jesus is controlling me. He's our saint that we pray to; that we look up to. Drug dealers, they sinning, right? But they'll be millionaires. How I got shot five times—only a saint, only Black Jesus, only a nigga that know where I'm coming from, could be, like, 'You know what? He's gonna end up doing some good.'"[46] There is a glimmer of hope, of possibility, implicit in the ethic promoted by Tupac because "by both rejecting and embracing suffering, Tupac offers a complex prayer that does not merely glorify violence but interrogates its meaning and howls at the pain it wrecks."[47] Perhaps Tupac's twist on an ethic of human endeavor reflects some of what Camus means when saying, "rebellion, without claiming to solve everything, can at least confront its problems," or when saying:

> Rebellion is born of the spectacle of irrationality, confronted with an unjust and incomprehensible condition. But its blind impulse is to demand order in the midst of chaos, and unity in the very heart of the ephemeral. It protests, it demands, it insists that the outrage be brought to an end, and that what has up to now been built upon shifting sands should henceforth be founded on rock. Its preoccupation is to transform. But to transform is to act, and to act will be, tomorrow, to kill, and it still does not know whether murder is legitimate. Rebellion engenders exactly the actions it is asked to legitimate. Therefore it is absolutely necessary that rebellion find its reasons within itself, since it cannot find them elsewhere. It must consent to examine itself in order to learn how to act.[48]

Tupac's theological formulations imply many of the basic dimensions of humanism. One might think of his perspective as a shift from a theistic orientation to a human-centered orientation, from a final appeal to transhistorical reality to a "comfort" with sensory experience as the limits of reality. It involves an epistemological stance signaling a determination to "claim a human situation in which all the answers are human—in other words, formulated in reasonable terms. From this moment every question, every word, is an act of rebellion while in the sacred world every word is an act of grace."[49] The discomfort more traditional religionists experience with Tupac's corpus speaks to the presence of humanistic principles, a perspective on humanity and human life that is often troubling. Michael Dyson provides an example of this when referring to evangelical minister T. D. Jakes, who spoke of Tupac as representing "a generation that had trodden underfoot the principles of God, leaving their ideas over God instead of God's ideas reigning over theirs."[50]

There are humanist sensibilities and assertions to be found in rap music—explicit and strong. Rap often points a direction; raises questions; advances a critique; and in the process speaks a late-twentieth-century and early twenty-first-century word of appreciation to human-centered accountability. To borrow from rapper Sage Francis, anything else would involve ridiculously "easy answers."[51]

On Profiling: A Humanist Interpretation of the "Fixing" of Black Bodies[1]

In this chapter, I provide another example of how humanist principles serve to frame a hermenuetic, a way of interpreting and reading texts and events.[2] I believe this exercise, begun in chapter five, is significant in that it provides a sense of an important dimension of humanism's function within African American communities. As opposed to simply thinking in terms of institutions and practices, this chapter, along with chapters five and seven, demonstrate that African Americans exercise humanist principles, as Black Christians use Christianity, also in the way they think about and interpret the world.

While a graduate student in Cambridge, Massachusetts, I was given the opportunity to teach a course at a local university—"The Philosophy of Race and Gender." Within the course I attempted to problematize gender and race. I thought one of the best ways to accomplish this with respect to race was to bring into question our ability to remove the structural (and personal) manifestations of racism. The text I used for this portion of the course was Derrick Bell's *Faces At The Bottom Of The Well*, the second of his conversations with, to, and through Counselor Crenshaw. Bell, with brilliant prose and stories, toys with the idea that prejudice is a permanent feature of U.S. society. And with this as the case what do we do?

This is a provocative idea, particularly in light of the mythic status of the Civil Rights Movement and its leadership. This period, the 60's and 70's, marked a tremendous sense of optimism. Those who participated on the "front lines" of social protest believed that genuine effort toward transformation, including personal sacrifice, would undoubtedly bring about the desired results. History moved toward a beneficial outcome and progress was more than possible for the devoted shapers of U.S. liberal agendas. There was, I suppose, reason for this optimism. Those involved saw change; perhaps not the ultimate renewal of life, but they experienced penultimate movements or liberating impulses that stimulate additional effort. They believed because they saw the fruit of their belief (and action). But what about those born during and after the conservative swing inaugurated by President Ronald Reagan, and after the socio/historical nadir solidified by the age of crack cocaine? For those within this group, commonly associated with "Generation X" (a less than useful categorization), belief based upon outcome seems dangerously naive. Within this group, the glory of the Civil Rights Movement is at best a rather sterile history lesson. This group has seen more socio-political and economic failure than success, at least this is how it appears. Such concerns bring into question some of our basic and progressive certainties about the movement of human life; we have believed—most of us anyway—that bad situations are correctable. But what if this is not the case? What then?

Humanism is uncomfortable with either perspective—the hyper optimism generated through the Civil Rights Movement and the hyper pessimism generated through the conservative backlash. Both are misleading.

Drawing from the principles framing this book, I suggest a reevaluation of success and progress that notes the possibility for transformation—in limited doses—presented by the former and a sense of the looming possibility of failure nurtured by the latter group (the post-Reagan group). History, accordingly, demonstrates human potential for transforming action but a legacy of oppression (i.e., racism, classism, sexism, ageism, homophobia, heterosexism, etc.) points to a tendency toward the demonic (life working against life) that is just as strong. As it stands, assumptions of guaranteed outcomes based upon genuine effort are no longer sustainable. We work toward liberation because we must, with an eye toward the process not toward a certain outcome. This perspective requires not only a rethinking of liberation, but also an analysis of the nature and meaning of power.

Power always manifests in relationships, and these relationships entail some having the ability to name, shape, and place others in accordance with the psychological and material needs of the dominant group. This ability, in fact, is the very definition of power. In the context of the United States, one of the most historically sustained examples of this involves the relationship between white Americans and black Americans, and the ability of the former to overdetermine or fix the identity of the latter, to reduce the importance and value of blacks to their physical bodies. This involves a reduction of blacks to "flesh", a substance, or object from which to forge history. I would like to address this topic through attention to an example of this fixing or overdetermining of black Americans[3]: profiling as a mode of fixing identity. My goal does not involve the presentation of alternate uses of power; rather, I am concerned with the outlining of power as a problem. Or to borrow from Foucault, I am interested in using African American experience as a way of discussing negative power modalities through which institutions and "reality" are developed. In this sense, power is both directed at and articulated through black bodies and their "placement".

The Black Body as an Arena for Power

Writing on the African context, in *Black Skin, White Masks*, Frantz Fanon uses his training in psychiatry to reflect on the consequences of racism on the black psyche. Fanon states that "this work represents the sum of the experiences and observations of seven years; regardless of the area I have studied, one thing has struck me: The Negro enslaved by his inferiority, the white man enslaved by his superiority alike behave in accordance with a neurotic orientation."[4] This relationship of assumed inferiority and proclaimed superiority results in certain depictions of blacks as having "no culture, no civilization, no 'long historical past.' "[5] Blacks become an oddity, a "something," an object.[6] Furthermore, there is a preoccupation with the black body as a marker of "something," as the storehouse for the fears, anxieties, stories, phobias, and desires of whites.

It is in this way that blacks are overdetermined or fixed in historical time and space. It accounts for the manner in which blacks are restricted and deprived of the ability to transcend their circumstances because their very being is said to be captured by their context. A process or "second creation" takes place through which humanity is exorcised and blacks are categorized into things to be used, worked, and discarded.[7] The only way to control the body and its usefulness as described above is to render it docile. In other words, "the body becomes a useful force only if it is both a productive body and a subjected body."[8]

Blacks had identity, but a truncated identity that did not significantly vary from the ambiguity of being forged during the period of slavery, for example. There was certainly difference, substantive difference, between the period of slavery and the post-slavery context. Nonetheless, both are defined by a form of subordination and violent suppression meant to maintain a certain racial order through the exercise of power. Slavery entailed blacks having no will, no purpose, outside that determined by owners. The Civil War fostered a paradigm shift in that whites were forced to think about blacks in terms of rights and liberties, but these remain circumscribed, and discussed primarily in terms of the ability to commit crimes and be punished accordingly. In short, blacks had to learn to be happy with the identity—as objects of history—given them. And those who failed to find this content-ment, or who gave the illusion of defiance, could easily face discipline and punishment as a way of containing the threat posed by black bodies "out of control". The threat of punishment and discipline has remained intact over the course of the twentieth century, although the methods for enactment have been "refined".

Color Consciousness: Profiling as an Exercise of Power

What is the look, the "color," of crime—the threat to security and the established way of life? While life in the United States provides numer-ous examples, post "9/11" develops have made profiling a much discussed topic. Questions have been raised over the nation's right to protect itself and its citizenry by highlighting for special attention and consideration those whose "look" and cultural aesthetics sound an alarm. Some might consider this a new conversation, arising out of twenty-first century terrorism on U.S. soil; yet it is much older and solidly lodged in the relationship between black Americans and the dominant society. An understanding of power as the ability to fix another's identity should include an awareness of racial profiling as another mode of power through which black Americans have been overdetermined and fixed. Racial profiling involves the overdetermi-nation or fixing of black identity in that it reduces those who encounter this exercise of power to a stereotypical arrangement of flesh vis-a-vis color and its socioeconomic and political ramifications.

According to Tracey Maclin, one can trace the roots of profiling "to a time in early American society when court officials in cities like Philadelphia permitted constables and ordinary citizens the right to 'take up' all black persons seen 'gadding abroad' without their master's permission. This means it transcends law enforcement and includes everyone—people like store clerks, bank tellers, security guards, and even taxi drivers."[9] A less vaguely articulated linking of slavery and post-slavery America with respect to racial profiling involves the connections between patrollers during the period of slavery who monitored the movement of blacks within the plantation system to law enforcement agents who monitor the movement of black bodies on roads and byways during the twentieth and twenty-first centuries. For example, compare the activity of profiling with this depiction of the night patrollers: "few figures loomed as large in the ex-slaves' memory as the patrollers, white men who policed the plantation countryside. These white men, often nonslaveholders, captured and punished slaves who ran away, took leave without a pass from their owner; violated curfews, or breached other laws or customs."[10] Blacks in this case were suspect simply because of their color. Potential guilt of criminal intent was premised strictly on the basis of fitting a profile, and a desire to restrict the mobility of black bodies. This practice, growing out of the practice of criminal profiling, has been maintained in the contemporary context of U.S. life. For example:

> Suron Jacobs, a construction worker in his twenties who is African American, had a construction job as part of a crew on a project in a nearly all-white suburban area outside Toledo, Ohio. One day, Jacobs made arrangements to meet his brother on a corner near the construction site during his lunch break to exchange an apartment key. Unbeknownst to Jacobs, a resident who saw him waiting on the corner for his brother called 911 and reported him as a suspicious person. Responding to the call, a police officer drove by, stopped, and began to question Jacobs. What was he doing? Where was his brother, and how long had he been waiting? Why was he in this neighborhood? After a number of these questions, Jacobs became irritated. He refused to answer any more questions and began walking back to the construction site. Jacobs immediately learned the price of defying the police in a place where 'he didn't belong'; the officer grabbed him, while another who had arrived on the scene handcuffed him.[11]

Those profiled are defined not in terms of a full range of complex possibilities and realities—moral outlook, social relationships and affiliations, political perspectives and activities, and so on. Rather, those in the position of power assume they know all there is to know about this person based upon external markers referred to as "CARD" or class, age, race (hence racial profiling), and dress.[12] They are reduced to a stereotype, and their life options are limited and suspended based on this judgment.

Some argue that profile-determined search is justified based on the high percentage of crimes committed by people of color, particularly blacks. Yet, as a 1995 case against the Maryland State Police uncovered, "when they searched a hundred blacks and a hundred whites, they found drugs exactly the same number of times, but they were searching seven hundred blacks for every one hundred whites, so the arrest statistics made it look like seventy percent of the people being arrested for drugs were African American, and then they use those statistics to justify focusing on the African Americans." It was also noted that roughly 72 percent of those stopped on I-95 were African American.[13] This deconstruction of the popular mythology regarding racial profiling is also present in the recent book by David A. Harris. He writes: "contrary to what the 'rational' law enforcement justification for racial profiling would predict, the hit rate for drugs and weapons in police searches of African Americans is the same as or lower than the rate for whites."[14]

I conclude with a return to Frantz Fanon because the manner in which physical appearance is used to capture the individual's essence and determine his/her worth, as an act of power, is brilliantly presented in his work. At one point this situation is symbolically summed up by the proclamation of a young child: "Look, a Negro!" This remark points to the otherness of the black within the context of a world defined by white superiority. In the words of Fanon, " . . . I am being dissected under white eyes, the only real eyes. I am fixed. Having adjusted their microtomies, they objectively cut away slices of my reality. I am laid bare. I feel, I see in those white faces that it is not a new man who has come in, but a new kind of man, a new genus. Why, it's a Negro!"[15] Such a sentiment is expressed, in more subtle but no less harmful ways, through the overdetermining of black identity—an exercising of power often couched in the language of law and social order.

Nimrod's Children Have Bodies: Humanist Sensibilities, Black Theology, and Sex(uality)[1]

In section III of this book, I have suggested that humanism serves as a hermeneutic by which various life events and historical moments are unpacked and understood. In this chapter, I continue my work with humanism as hermeneutic and apply it to a vexing issue—sex(uality). Giving primary attention to the humanist principle of human central-ity and the sense of irreverence that marks the legacy of Nimrod, I chronicle the negative tension between religiosity and sexuality in the context of black religion and black theology. My goal is to present the nature of this tension and offer a way of better addressing sex(uality) within the context of black religious life and thought.[2] I begin this discussion with attention to the historical context for current notions of black sex(uality).

The "Shaping" of Black Sex(uality)

Only intensified by the ramifications of a legacy of disregard for black bodies, the tension between religious devotion and physical pleasure is old. Furthermore, it is deeply embedded in the practice and teachings of the Christian faith and at times tied to scientific pronouncements. For example, in nineteenth-century United States some within scien-tific circles argued that "desire by itself 'disturbs and disorders all the functions of the system,'" and an orgasm "stimulated the 'convulsed heart' to drive blood 'in fearful congestion, to the principal viscera,' damag[ed] all other organs."[3] The negative weight of science served to dampen, so to speak, the individual's relationship to her or his body. However, the dilemma is much older than pre-twentieth-century medical speculation in that it marked sexual sensibilities in Europe and the Americas as of the age of exploration. (It is important to note that it was during this period that Christianity "splintered within Europe" and came into contact with other cultural and religious sensibilities in the "New World."[4]) Christianity certainly did not invent this problematic relationship to sex(uality) but there are ways in which the Christian faith highlighted theologically in negative terms humans as sexual entities and gave believers the mission of undermining or undoing their sexual selves.

Christian faith's (along with secular authorities') regulation of sex(uality) eventually gave raise to new perspectives on the body and what is commonly referred to as "modern sexuality," marked by new ways of controlling and in some instances "denaturalizing" and discourse-enveloping sex(uality) and sexual life.[5] As "modern sexuality" develops it does so with respect to growing notions of and perceptions of race and racial difference. That is to say, "imperial power is explicitly and implicitly linked with sexuality . . . imperial powers shaped cultural constructions of masculinity and femininity and how images of colonial peoples were gendered and sexualized."[6] It will be important to remember during the course of this discussion that bodies are constructed, shaped, and positioned, and that much of this activity is sexed and deeply connected to matters of pleasure and pleasuring.

Within the framework of imperial developments and conquest in North America, the black body represented the physical world of work and pleasure and also served as a prime symbol of chaos. In either case, in physical terms or as symbolic representation, those of African descent were something both appealing and repulsive. As an ontological and epistemological challenge, black bodies were controlled through relegation to subhuman status and the violent forms of control and linguistic determination that such an indictment allowed. Hence the individual African's activities and patterns of conduct were shaped by and served to reenforce the larger symbolic frame work of society. Nonetheless, it should be noted that interracial relationships in the "New World" occurred early and often. But physical intimacy did not mean that the "Other"—those of African descent—held equal status with those of European descent. In fact, race and class distinctions were reinforced through theories of sexuality—sexual restrictions and regulations. The enslaved (and free) person of African descent was named and "known." While understood as irrational and of lesser value, Africans in North America were sufficient fodder for slave holder's erotic pathologies and the general sexual release of any white person who desired black flesh.

Enslaved Africans in this sense, both men and women, became accept-able repositories for sexual desires and repulsions because subduing the racial other in the "New World" implied the ability to sexually have them. Black bodies were considered, in Foucaultian terms, "saturated with sex."[7] The genitals of the African, hence, were both threatening and desirable. So sexual and sexualized were they that sex became the prime marker of their reality and meaning from the perspective of pro-slavery whites. Through erotic imagination and sexual conquest of enslaved Africans (male and female) both sexual and racial difference were addressed and order maintained, with the added benefit of physi-cal pleasure for the conqueror.

M. Shawn Copeland notes with great insight that "European and European American representative aesthetics scaled, identified, and labeled the bodies of black women as primitive, lascivious, and repug-nant. This evaluation was at once religious and moral." That is to say, "it reflected both white Western Christianity's ambivalence toward the body, sex, as well as sexuality, and the impact of religion on what Kelly Brown Douglas refers to as the construction and 'management of sexual discourse,' thus fostering the 'domination and demonization of the different Other.'"[8] Put another way, during the period of slavery, those of African descent were painted sexual savages who operated based on the satisfying of unnaturally strong desires. As a consequence, they were incapable of proper social relationships with whites and had to be controlled to avoid social chaos.[9] Interestingly enough, one mechanism of control was sexual contact. Linda Brent's *Incidents in the Life of a Slave Girl: An Authentic Historical Narrative Describing the Horrors of Slavery as Experienced by Black Women*, for example, speaks to the manner in which enslaved African women faced the threat of unwanted sexual contact with whites. She says the following concerning her master's plans to make her his mistress:

> When my master said he was going to build a house for me, and that he could do it with little trouble and expense, I was in hopes something would happen to frustrate his scheme; but I soon heard that the house was actually begun. I vowed before my Maker that I would never enter it. I had rather toil on the plantation from dawn till dark; I had rather live and die in jail, than drag on, from day to day, through such a living death. I was determined that the master, whom I so hated and loathed, who had blighted the prospects of my youth, and made my life a desert, should not, after my long struggle with him, succeed at last in trampling his victim under his feet. I would do any thing, every thing, for the sake of defeating him. What *could* I do?[10]

Brent made an effort to maintain some control over her body and the pleasure it gave others. Yet, the system of slavery allowed little space for assertions of self. There was for those of African descent a feeling that one always stands the chance of losing oneself to others. One easily becomes an object to be manipulated for the satisfaction of others, which involves an ontological and existential slide into nothingness except for the pleasure one's body can give others.

Sex was a ritual through which white men, for instance, maintained the established social order, but for black women it was a terror to be escaped as best they could. Albeit Brent could not choose to avoid sexual contact, she could decide with whom to have such contact. This is a valuable move from her perspective because:

> ... to be an object of interest to a man who is not married, and who is not her master, is agreeable to the pride and feelings of a slave, if her miserable situation has left her any pride or sentiment. It seems less degrading to give one's self, than to submit to compulsion. There is something akin to freedom in having a lover who has no control over you, except that which he gains by kindness and attachment.[11]

During the period of slavery, black flesh formed bodies that mattered in only a limited sense and for limited purposes, all revolving around the pleasuring of whites—economically, socially, physically. The genitalia of these black bodies, then, was enlarged or given extreme attention and importance over against the deeper ontological reality of blacks.[12]

Sex and sex(uality) became modes of regulation and, in this way, Judith Butler remarks, served to not only control but also create bodies. In part through a discourse of sexuality, whites developed a story or language of black being that had materiality and that "call[ed] into being" both a type of black body and a type of white body. This process entailed restrictions on the "existence" and movement of both types of bodies, and also the ability to recognize the ontological depth both might shadow.[13] This paradoxical activity of "fondling" and fixing involves both a process of construction (the making of these bodies) and deconstruction (a perverting of meaning that might be associated with the subjects represented by those bodies).[14] In a sense, discourse of sexuality became ritualized annihilation—a controlling of bodies—that provided whites (and some blacks) with psychological and physical pleasure that was orgasmic (i.e., gratifying) on the level of the individual and the social.

After slavery sexual aggression such as rape and sexual mutilation (e.g., castration during lynching) continued the process of sexualization as affirmation of the status quo. Frantz Fanon speaks to this preoccupation with black bodies as radically sexual when connecting the hatred of whites for blacks to sexuality. He says, "since his [the white man's] ideal is an infinite virility, is there not a phenomenon of diminution in relation to the Negro, who is viewed as a penis symbol? Is the lynching of the Negro not a sexual revenge? We know how much of sexuality there is in all cruelties, tortures, beatings."[15] Through the physical destruction of black body parts that symbolize threat (and source of potential and often forbidden pleasure), sexuality provided another powerful means by which whites maintained control over people of color. As R. W. Connell remarks, "cultural hierarchies of bodies are robust."[16]

Controlling bodies had to entail regulation of sexual desire to the extent sex(uality) acted out through flesh had ramifications for all spaces occupied by (or denied to) these bodies. As we shall see, religion and theological discourse served as useful tools in sexually policing bodies because "while people struggle to find life and meaning in the relationships of the sofa beds of friends and lovers, systematic theology struggles to master and obliterate those meanings."[17]

Religious Reinforcement of Imposed Black Sex(uality)

In the North American colonies, Puritan sensibilities played an important role in the formation of conservative attitudes toward sex and sexuality, by which activities such as anal intercourse and masturbation, for instance, were deemed great evils to be avoided without exception. While the rhetoric was strong, actual punishment for sodomy was rare. According to one source, "there were about twenty sodomy prosecutions in British North America, of which two ended in hanging, both in the 17th century. . . . Because sodomy convictions required proof of penetration and testimony of two witnesses, they were extremely difficult to prove. . . ."[18] A preoccupation with the unruly nature of the body and the dangerous nature of its desires and pleasures would spread in the colonies through the two Great Awakenings, the first in the 1700s and the second in the 1800s.

Even earlier than this period within the context of Christianity, religion and sexuality were understood "as a binary opposition."[19] This, of course, stems from the manner in which the Christian faith placed in direct relationship the spirit of God and human flesh, most pronouncedly in the Christ event. This, however, is a Christ who remains rather sexless. And what the followers of Christ through the centuries gather from this event is an understanding of the body as a reluctant and difficult partner for the spirit. Ethicist Emilie Townes in a discussion of health and caring, puts it this way, "when we live out of an incarnational understanding that takes us out of the *dynamic* dualism we have of body *and* spirit, then we lapse into the *deadly* dualism that tells us that the body is inferior, if not evil, and must be transcended by the spirit of Jesus."[20] Recall the sentiment of Apostle Paul paraphrased here: That which I would not do, I do.

The flesh fights the deeper desires of the spirit and in this way makes difficult meaningful connection to the divine. In a sense, those who are Christlike are required to overcome the flesh, to subdue its desires and pleasures for the sake of spiritual connection to the divine. One might say that "it is Augustine's fear and loathing of the sexual body that has determined the entire course of Christian history."[21] Later figures such as Martin Luther gave importance to sex within the context of marriage. This, however, did not entail a recognition of sex as good. Rather, it was seen, even if it did not produce children, as a necessary component of married life. Yet, like the Apostle Paul, Luther and other major figures in the Protestant denominations gave more weight to a spiritual existence over and above that of marriage.[22] Religious communities continue into the twenty-first century to teach "a sexual code based on fear of the body and of sexuality, in understandings of sexual virtue as the repression of bodily desires by the force of the rationale will, on physicality, especially sexuality, as an obstacle to spirituality. . . ."[23]

The oppressive nature of life in the United States combined with adherence to traditional Christian perceptions of the flesh and sex(uality) resulted in alienation from the body—particularly the body as erotic and sexual and even more so with respect to homosexuality and other modes of pleasuring the body outside established sexual norms. Judith Butler speaks to this when reflecting on the work of Hazel Carby. Carby remarks that the vulnerability of black women's bodies that continues into the twentieth century, "including rape, because their bodies continued to be sites of conquest within white racism, then the psychic resistance to homosexuality and to a sexual life outside the parameters of the family must be read in part as a resistance to an endangering public exposure."[24] Race and sex(uality) mark each other, play off each other, inform each other in the context of the United States. Preoccupation with spiritual renewal meant suspicion concerning attention to the body and, being mindful of this, Christians were encouraged to avoid sexual sins of all kinds.

For black churches religious tradition/scriptures and the desire to gain for blacks recognition as morally and ethically meriting full inclusion in society generated participation in the prevailing attitudes towards sex(uality). Nonetheless it is important to remember that an embrace of societal and religious sexual norms was both active (based on reading of and adherence to biblical tradition) and reactionary (based on a desire for social inclusion). This tension between race and sex(uality) is vividly and creatively described in literary depictions of black religiosity.

Larsen and Baldwin on Religion and Sex(uality)

There is an uncomfortable sexual quality to the movements and language of many black religious practices and aesthetics. Just exactly how awkward or unwanted this sexual dimension can be is expressed by writer Nella Larsen. Helga Crane, the protagonist in *Quicksand*, stumbles upon a religious meeting during a period of personal angst. While pleasurable on some level, Helga's encounter with black worship is also terrifying in that it momentarily mutates existing boundaries by reasserting the visibility of black bodies. Yet this occurs without there being a full escape from the hierarchal structures and norms of the social environment. It entails a movement forward by ritually moving back. Nella Larsen describes Helga's experience this way:

> Fascinated, Helga Crane watched until there crept upon her an indistinct horror of an unknown world. She felt herself in the presence of a nameless people, observing rites of a remote obscure origin. The faces of the men and women took on the aspect of a dim vision. "This," she whispered to herself, "is terrible. I must get out of here." But the horror held her. She remained motionless, watching, as if she lacked the strength to leave the place—foul, vile, and terrible, with its mixture of breaths, its contact of bodies, its conceited convulsions, all in wild appeal for a single soul. Her soul. And as Helga watched and listened, gradually a curious influence penetrated her; she felt an echo of the weird orgy resound in her own heart; she felt herself possessed by the same madness; she too felt a brutal desire to shout and to sling herself about.[25]

There are implications to the tension present in Helga Crane's life. Her experiences of attraction and repulsion regarding the sexualized qualities of human life are not simply a matter of Larsen exercising literary license. Rather, Helga's experience speaks to long-standing opposition between religious perceptions of the body and the sexual dimensions of human interaction that is also expressed in the work of James Baldwin.

Baldwin, near the end of *Go Tell It On the Mountain*, provides a scene that merges the religious and physical, psychological and emotional experiences framing the development of protagonist John Grimes. John is on the floor of the Pentecostal church he and his family attend "wrestling" with the call of God and the demands of surrender to God's will. He has been "slain" by the Spirit. And while in this position, prostrate on the floor, John rehearses in his mind the tension between spirit and flesh, between the religious rhetoric and posture of his stepfather, a preacher—but "being a preacher ain't never stopped a nigger from doing his dirt"[26]—and the erotic activities that seem to run contrary to all things holy:

> And I *heard* you—all the nighttime long. I know what you do in the dark, black man, when you think the Devil's son's [John] asleep. I heard you spitting, and groaning, and choking—and I *seen* you, riding up and down, and going in and out. I ain't the Devil's son for nothing. . . . And I hate you. I hate you. I don't care about your golden crown. I don't care about your long white robe. I seen you under the robe. I seen you![27]

There is something fundamental—intrinsic—in this tension between spirit and flesh that tortured John as he lay on the floor of that church. It was not simply that John wrestled with the sexual self within the context of a religious tradition that despised the generic human body. It was not just any body that was despised. It was his black body, a body condemned, according to certain interpretations of scripture, by God through Noah's son Ham and Ham's son, Canaan. It was his body, complete with its desires and sexual interests.

John, and many blacks, feel this assumed stain and it is only intensified through a recognition of the body as sexualized—a sort of double condemnation.[28] On the floor voices bombarded John, framing harsh questions through indirect appeal to Genesis 9:

> then the ironic voice, terrified, it seemed, of no depth, no darkness, demanded of John, scornfully, if he believed that he was cursed. All niggers had been cursed, the ironic voice reminded him, all niggers had come from this most undutiful of Noah's sons. How could John be cursed for having seen in a bathtub [John saw his father naked in the tub as alluded to in the quotation above] what another man—if that other man had ever lived—had seen ten thousand years ago, in an open tent?[29]

John seeing his father naked in the tub and the epistemological link with Ham assumed in the above quotation did not generate feelings of comfort with the sexual self. Rather, what stems from recognition of sexual potential for the religious person is a desire to reject or "hide" from the body. There is expressed during those long moments on the floor the difficulty of carrying one's flesh through this world, while searching for a way to heaven. This God John wrestles with created flesh, but seems to despise it and, what is more, seems to require followers to also despise those things the body yearns for. The theology and practice of John's church push toward dysfunction and sexual pathology in the form of "crosses" gladly carried by the righteous. As Michael Lynch notes in his analysis of Go Tell It On the Mountain, a "religious neurosis" marks the characters of the book. It is a neurosis through which "temporal happiness and spiritual redemption are seemingly impossible attainments—largely because," as Baldwin notes through the somewhat autobiographical character John Grimes, "they are seen as antithetical terms of a dichotomy."[30]

The body expresses its desires and needs regardless, although the strictures of the Church, according to Baldwin's account, amplify either the rejection of sex(uality) or the lurid embrace of the same. As work on racial identity done by Anthony Appiah and Amy Gutman might suggest if applied to Baldwin's book, John's struggle for meaning expressed throughout the novel shows that identity (including the erotic self) is informed by a complex of perspectives and opinions, many of them forged through sensibilities made available by cultural organizations such as religion.[31] In this sense, one might say that the black church, in John's case the Pentecostal church, seeks to control sex(uality) through a process of "enclosure" whereby the adherent is cut off from her or his body and the larger world.[32] What results are "life scripts" giving shape to every aspect of movement through the world—social sensibilities, political perspectives, attitudes toward the sexual and erotic, and so on.[33] This strict mapping out of life is not unusual, as James Nelson remarks, because sex(uality), for example, is believed to have a power that religion fears and seeks to monitor and restrict.[34]

Questioning of these life guidelines results in guilt and anxiety that mar relationships to one's body and the bodies of others.[35] Such a situation is existentially and ontologically debilitating: Does such an arrangement entail life? Is this to live, to really live, to make one's mark on the world? To the contrary, movement through the world motivated by a rejection of one's body—what one's body gives and enjoys—is to exist barely. In this way, the beauty of the black body, something Baldwin through John seeks to experience, is at best a hauntingly tragic beauty—something one must acknowledge and celebrate only in the darkened corners of one's mind and historical spaces, all the time aware that sexual "sin" leaves a deep and persistent stain. Pleasure within the context of such an antibody religious environment yields something depressingly short of freedom from the terror of existence in an absurd world. As Vivian May remarks, "through John's transgressions, Baldwin indirectly portrays how fundamental the church has been in defining and controlling sexuality. Baldwin demonstrates that social and cultural pressures affect how we pursue and acquire the trappings of identity."[36]

In reflecting on the religious environment in which John struggles for life, Baldwin makes a theological shift, suggesting in soft tones that salvation need not entail the rejection of one's body. Rather, the ability to love oneself and others through erotic love is the marker of salvation.[37] This erotic quality is continuously pushed below the surface, but hinted at or teased through the sway of spirit possession or the knowing/unknowing moments of bodily contact as the devout of God embrace at the end of a powerful service. But can spiritualized pleasure fulfill the ache of bodily desire? Baldwin left the Church in order to find salvation so conceived. Yet, how does one—can one— secure salvation as he understands it within the context of traditional religious community? Is the Black Church capable of embracing a more complex and inclusive notion of sex(uality) and sexual pleasure?

Embodiment as New Possibility

Perhaps the most complete critique in black religious studies of black churches on this score is found in Kelly Brown Douglas's *Sexuality and the Black Church*.[38] In this text Douglas argues that God's revelation has weighty consequences for an understanding of and appreciation for sex(uality).

Black churches may have encountered a warped theory of sex(uality) as part of "the White cultural assault upon [black] sexuality," but unlike other harmful ideologies received (e.g., inferiority of blacks) it was embraced and refined within the context of black community discourse as a non-discourse, as a modality of control in that ideological penetration of sex(uality) affects one's total reality as historical being in that "sexuality implies one's very humanity."[39] (Again, the sexual ethics and norm of the black churches is a result of an active/reactive process.) Douglas seeks to balance this depiction of sex(uality) as a reaction to white discourse with a sense of blacks as forging more positive and "healthy" notions of their sexual selves. In essence, Douglas argues that the exploitation and manipulation of black sex(uality) has harnessed black bodies, making and shaping them in ways that result in a discomfort on the part of blacks with their bodies and their sexual selves. In turn, black theological discourse responds with an immature rhetoric that in no way resembles the more hearty discourse on, for instance, socioeconomic realities. In a word, sex(uality) became a "taboo issue" for both black churches and black theology.[40]

Over the course of centuries, the sex(uality) of blacks has been mutated and amplified in the popular imagination of the United States, Douglas laments. This being the case, how then, could blacks develop a discourse on sex(uality) that did not run the risk of being warped and used to buttress stereotypes that assume blacks are always thinking about sex? Rather than run the risk of having such a discussion backfire, blacks, Douglas notes, have preferred to avoid public discourse on sex(uality).[41] While one might see this as a troubling silence that supports homophobia and other problematic attitudes and perspectives, and one that feeds a continuing discomfort with black bodies, Douglas suggests that one might also see this as a "form of Black cultural resistance to the corrupting influences of White culture, or a survival strategy against White cultural attacks."[42]

I agree with Douglas's argument that sex(uality) is an essential component of theology for black religious expression, if the centrality of embodiment as the marker of human-divine relationship is to be maintained. Such is the case because, and again I agree with Douglas, "to manifest our loving relationship to God is to be in a loving relationship with God's creation," thereby rendering attitudes such as homophobia an act of bad faith—a break with "authentic Black faith."[43] There is merit to Douglas's analysis, although I would give greater emphasis to the active role blacks have played in promoting a warped depiction of sexuality. But this is not the first issue blacks have failed to address adequately. The same was the case, for example, with sexism and classism. However, correctives have been offered with regard to these ideological oversights while little attention has been given to breaking this harmful silence on the part of blacks in general and black religious institutions in particular.

This much is clear: blacks in general and black religionists in particular have advocated harmful policies regarding sex(uality). Such policies are expressed, for instance, in the framing of rather conservative notions of femininity and masculinity as normative. In turn these normative notions reinforce sexism through a restriction on the spaces in which women rightly operate (e.g., regulations against ordained ministry) and homophobia through an ideology of homosexuality as conspiracy against the black family. One example of this practice within religious circles must suffice here. I provide this statement elsewhere and again here because of the manner in which it frames the black church's complicity in promoting myopic gender arrangements. Reflecting on the appeal of a black church in Baltimore, a member said black men typically stay away from church because:

> the image of Christ is "wimpish" and encourages black men to "turn the other cheek" in response to racial injustice; that the traditions of "blond and blue-eyed" images of Christ reflect blacks' self-hatred and capitulation to white supremacy; that religious services are too emotionally driven because the churches are dominated by women, who "by nature" are emotional; and that, unlike the Nation of Islam, which among many unchurched men represents the essence of black manhood, black churches attract homosexuals.[44]

In response and as a way of attracting "men" to black churches, some promote an irresponsibly "muscular" message, one that enables overtly homophobic postures such as that presented by Goldie Phillips, a member of Bethel AME Church in Baltimore. He remarks that "under Pastor Reid's charge, they cannot look at Christianity as sissified . . . If they belong to this church and they've been studying under him for any time, impossible to view it like that [sic]. The brothers who come to church, they need to be touched, I mean physically touched. They need to know that they can maintain their macho manhood, but they can be touched."[45]

It should go without saying that such a perspective wherever found is problematic and should be challenged on every front. Douglas notes this, but attempts to maintain sympathy toward the manner in which blacks have fought for identity and integrity within an absurd social environment in ways that might counter efforts to hold blacks and their churches accountable and responsible for their troubling attitudes toward sex(uality). She writes, "the case supporting homophobia," for example, "in the Black community reveals homophobia almost as a misguided strategy for protecting Black lives and the integrity of Black sexuality, as a necessary position to safeguard Black life and freedom."[46]

It is not difficult to uncover the manner in which such a posture, even if a matter of survival, is far from effective in that it fosters a rather limited theory of relationship in which only certain types of activities provide acceptable arrangements of pleasure. While this may entail "the safeguard[ing of] Black life and freedom" to a certain extent, it does not allow for the type of individual and group "cultural fulfillment,"[47] as Victor Anderson names liberation, that appreciates sexual difference as a part of the mosaic of black life. That is to say, freedom is available only to those who love in a certain way because black sex(uality) is given fundamental dynamics that require adherence to normative frameworks in order to secure recognition and approval.

In an odd twist, many blacks, and certainly those within conservative church circles, attempted to "save" black bodies through a proscription of the ways in which these bodies could be displayed and put into relationship. Nonetheless, by celebrating the heterosexual norm, blacks have in fact reasserted racial hierarchy. Racial difference and sexual difference are worked out by negating the latter to safeguard the racial community. Bodily pleasure outside these accepted modalities involves sin because it entails a misuse or abuse of the body. While religious institutions such as black churches should have worked to elevate estrangement—to celebrate the body and the ways in which the body gives and receives sexual pleasure—they have actually reinforced a troubling body–spirit dichotomy. And this has been aided by black theological discourse's relative silence.

Reformulations: Step One

It is in this sense, following anthropologist Mary Douglas, one might think of religious experience and behavior as transmitting culture through the proscription of certain social relations and behaviors expressed in and through the body as symbol of the social system. The body, then, as a physical reality capable of receiving and giving sexual pleasure is recognized as "a highly restricted medium of expression," restricted by the larger social system.[48] An orgasm in a sense becomes a prime recognition of restriction in that it points to the body's goodness but also its profound limitations in that this release is a "little death." One might even consider the orgasm interpretable as sexual *communitas* by which I mean the less pleasurable realities of social existence are suspended and overwhelmed by a joy that cannot be maintained long term.

The subtle emphasis on relationship, as a useful hermeneutical shift, in my discussion of sex(uality) should suggest the manner in which I mean more than just actions, more than the "physical structure of the act or the status of those engaged in the act. . . ."[49] Hence sex(uality) becomes more than what individuals and groups do with or to each other. I want to hold in creative tension actions that preoccupy the teachings of religious institutions and more fundamental dynamics that escape their attention. In a word, I am not concerned with wrestling over what is "sinful" and what isn't as a way of doing battle with judgments stemming from an attitude of "sexual moral minimalism"[50] by which less sex and a tame sense of sex(uality) is more in keeping with the demands of the religious life. More important than this is a rethinking of the theological value of relationship in ways that affirm sex(uality) and the erotic as expression of complex modalities of interaction. Rather than simply seeking to have certain sexual behaviors once despised included in the array of accepted and appreciated modalities of pleasuring, I suggest a new understanding of relationship as a more fundamental or elemental attack on warped notions of the body and its encounters with others. In this way one is able to connect agape, philia, and eros in a web of interaction focused on the growth of complex patterns of exchange, celebrating the ways in which the body gives and receives sexual and non-sexual pleasure through a variety of experiences.

If black theology urges the bringing of one's experiences to scripture and tradition, in what way is the excluding of the sexual dimensions of life justified? Black theology must become a materialistic theology, one that has its "starting point in people's actions, or sexual acts without polarizing the social from the symbolic. It is from human sexuality that theology starts to search and understand the sacred, and not vice versa."[51] Black theology becomes a proper body theology to the extent it seeks to give priority to the bodily experiences of African Americans, moving from those experiences out to the world and, for theists, the transcendent. Such a theology is in essence "a celebration of embodiment beyond all definitions, enjoying a body for its own sake. It is an attempt to allow people to be framed by their bodies and not by culture or doctrine."[52]

The body has importance because it is, for the black theist, the vessel through which God's gift of sex(uality) flows. In this sense, resistance to dehumanization is present in that the body becomes an important and vital mode of expressing God and God's love to the world. With this said, one must ask a question: Is it possible to "celebrate, affirm, and experience . . . sexuality fully" within the context of traditional black Christianity? The embodied nature of the Christ event guarantees that Christ had a penis. Recognition of this, regardless of countless works of art that ignore it, is not a major break with inadequate theological discourse on sex(uality). Certainly Jesus was sensual, but *how* sensual and in what ways? This issue is not so easily resolved by shouting "Jesus had a penis!" (In fact this might create other problems.) The more radical question involves what he did with it? Was it erect? Did it serve as an outlet for pleasure for either men or women, or both? Through such questions we better gauge who Jesus was in human flesh, the divine housed in a body like ours. Such questions are uncomfortable, if not considered irreverent; but is that a bad thing?

These questions are more easily answered with respect to the gods of African-derived traditions present in black communities. The god's of Africa—orishas and lwas—are sexual without apologies, but for Christians such a recognition with regard to Christ has been unspeakable. As a consequence, the wholeness sought by black Christianity has been compromised through a rejection of certain dimensions of bodily experience. That is to say, "Christianity is an incarnational religion that claims to set captives free, it tells us it is a religion of liberation. Yet it underpins many of the restrictive practices that body politics expose."[53] Black theology, if it is to correct its inadequate discourse on sexuality, must "encourage people to express freedom and eroticize their equality."[54] This involves a new perspective on the part of black theologians by which they push themselves and religious communities to recognize and enjoy the ways in which bodies move in and through the world.

Section IV

Toward the Development of Black Humanist Studies

From my 30th year on I have increasingly regarded the church as an institution which defended such evils as slavery, color caste, exploitation of labor and war. I think the greatest gift of the Soviet Union to modern civilization was the dethronement of the clergy and the refusal to let religion be taught in the public schools.

—W. E. B. DuBois

Various essays and books have been written dealing with aspects of black humanism (defined in numerous ways). However, something resembling a modality of study has yet to develop with black humanism as its object of concern. The various essays and books published over the years point in the direction of such a mode of study, but suggest only in rough form the historical development of what I call black humanist studies. These materials and their various authors point to the black intellectual tradition from which black humanist studies must draw. They provide groundwork for a push toward a language and interdisciplinary approach for thinking through the African American presence in American life, highlighting the meaning of black humanism within this context (both the benefits and warts associated with this brand of humanist engagement).

Toward Black Humanist Studies Part One: Theological Discourse Reconceived

A Brief Opening Statement

In order to avoid confusion, I begin with an opening statement concerning the nature of black humanist studies. I understand that this statement is really much too short to qualify as a full chapter; yet, I also recognize that it's importance overrules the consideration of length.

I am not suggesting that black humanist studies should develop as a singular framework of theories and methods devoted to the understanding of African American experience. Rather, black humanist studies, like other approaches such as Cultural Studies and African American Studies, should be understood as an array of theoretical and methodological formulations—which experience shifts and changes—that respond to the changing nature of and meaning of African American life. There will be disagreement over the nature of black humanist studies. However, even such disagreements, arising from the various discourses housed within the framework of black humanist studies, help to shape the field in important ways.

With this said, there are basic dimensions to what I propose as black humanist studies that should be noted. First, the *black humanist* within black humanist studies refers to an arrangement of principles and sensibilities as outlined earlier in this volume. The object of black humanist studies is the language, "texts," beliefs, and activities of life lived in accordance with humanist principles. In a word, black humanist studies should be understood as the study of black humanism—the black humanist experience—as a way of being and thinking. It entails a certain type of philosophical positioning with ramifications that influence one's sense of self and one's relationship to the world.

Black humanist studies is concerned with mapping and understanding the ways in which African Americans (and this should expand to include Africa and other locations within the African diaspora) push for greater subjectivity, for more complex consciousness. Black humanist studies might be informed by existentialism, particularly as it has developed within the context of thought within the African diaspora. From existentialism, black humanist studies could easily gain a language for exploring the sense of the struggle for meaning in an absurd world that marks African American life. Furthermore, from thinkers such as Fanon, black humanist studies can secure a deep appreciation for the importance of the physical body in understanding the nature and development of African American identity and subjectivity. Fanon reminds black humanist studies that history is played out on and through dark bodies, and that the "placement" and depiction of these bodies has consequences for the political, social, economic, psychological, emotional, and religious development of life.

Black humanist studies is interested in description and analysis of the ways in which some African Americans form and practice identity in and in opposition to history, always mindful of how African American life develops within a context marred by racism, classism, sexism, and other forms of oppression as well as opportunities for growth and renewal. Black humanist studies must reject the metanarrative of African American life whereby a rather narrow range of philosophical perspectives and ideological commitments is considered worthy of analysis. Through a challenging of standard perceptions of African American life, black humanist studies keeps alive a central question: What does it mean to be African American, and what are the modalities of expressivity and constraint related to such an identity?

As part of this process of analysis, black humanist studies must avoid celebration at the expense of critique and critique at the expense of celebration of African American achievements. This must involve diligence on both the internal and external levels. By this I mean black humanist studies must question unrealistic claims made within black America as well as faulty assumptions made by those outside the immediate African American community. This proposed field of study must be done mindful of the warning Henry Louis Gates, Jr. provides concerning the nature of African American Studies: "but scholars are citizens, too, and if it is wrongheaded to demand political payoff from basic research, it would be equally untenable to demand that research be quarantined from the real-world considerations that weigh so heavily upon us." Openness to a multiplicity of intellectual and political possibilities should mark black humanist studies.[1]

Black humanist studies is political to the extent it seeks to present an accurate depiction of African American life and thought, done in ways that strike against various modalities of oppression—whether they be generated internally (within black America) or externally. One might think of this posture in black humanist studies, for example, through the manner in which figures such as James Forman made use of humanist principles and sensibilities as the philosophical ground-work for their community involvements. Or, one might think of the manner in which humanist principles seem to have influenced J. Saunder Reddings critique of the oppressive tendencies in American culture.

To undertake this work, black humanist studies must make use of a variety of approaches, a number of tools—undoubtedly borrowed from African American Studies, Cultural Studies, Religious Studies, and so on. I hold no illusion that what I propose here will offer the theoretical foundation for black humanist studies as an interdisciplinary approach, but it is my hope that it will encourage additional work—more content—in this area.[2]

I take an initial step toward the development of black humanist studies by proposing a humanist theological discourse that takes seriously the praxis and theoretical concerns of black humanism, and that serves as one method of investigation or approach—one dimension of the field—framing black humanist studies.[3] While what is stated in this chapter is far from sufficient for the full and systematic development of this theological discourse, this space does serve to provide an initial outline of several of the key components of this theology. Simply put, my thesis is this: humanism entails a form of African American religious experience that is vital but not adequately articulated through traditional Black theology. Hence, I suggest a Theology of Immanence that articulates a non-God based religious experience, drawn from the African American experience and committed to liberation through an ethic marked by continual struggle for full humanity. I present this thesis through loose attention to basic propositions: (1) religious experience as the quest for complex subjectivity; (2) theology as articulation of struggle for complex subjectivity; (3) community as ultimate concern; (4) human development as theological norm.[4]

Black and womanist theology of liberation have often demonstrated a concern with existential questions. And these existential questions have fostered challenges to traditional theological discourse related to God's perspective on issues of racism, sexism, and classism.[5] What has resulted from this discourse is a modified theism and, through a hermeneutic of suspicion and turn to empiricism, a rethinking of super-naturalism and eschatology.[6] Underlying this work is an assertion that the problem is one of language describing God not God's existence. In other words, religious language is considered inadequate for "knowl-edge" of God, and it can be manipulated to support the "status quo." The challenge, then, is to properly understand and articulate God's presence in the world in what Dwight Hopkin's labels the "spirit of liberation" that is for us, with us, and in us.[7] Black theology has traditionally understood religious experience as identity or subjectivity discovered, a renewing of connection with a divine reality. God, in this form of theology, is the center of the human quest for identity and meaning because God has continuously demonstrated a concern with the securing of freedom or full humanity for the oppressed. Black theol-ogy points to scripture as well as African American material culture for affirmations of this claim. This is where I differ.

I suggest there is nothing behind the symbol God and, furthermore, this symbol is inadequate in light of African American history and cur-rent needs. Hence, I argue for religious experience not as an encounter with the divine, but rather as the creation of identity or complex subjectivity (realization of full humanity), understood in terms of the individual *and* community. In this sense, religious experience entails a human response to a crisis of identity (or, objectification), and it is the crisis of identity or "being" that constitutes the dilemma of ultimacy and meaning. The religious is a certain "ordering" or "style"of experi-ence as opposed to a unique form of experience; it is a paradigm shift or perspective. So conceived, religious experience is historically situ-ated and culturally bound—dealing with "the material world of outer nature" and "the human world of social life."[8]

Religious experience as outlined here is religious in that it addresses the search for ultimate meaning also called complex subjectivity. It is humanistic in that this ultimate meaning does not entail a transcendence *beyond* this world and it is African American because it is shaped by and within the context of African American historical realities and cultural creations. Ultimacy here is understood as a certain quality of finite relationship called "community." On this point I agree with Sharon Welch: Ultimate orientation in this experience is guided by a quality of relationship that replaces, in function and meaning, the tradi-tional notion of "God" or the "gods."[9] This turn from "God" or "gods" is designed to "free minds and bodies of a subjugated people."[10]

My concern with community as a mediating factor, the way in which the individual is "humbled" and connected to a larger existence and held accountable, keeps my perspective from being mere religious solipsism. When subjectivity is considered in light of community, tendencies toward extreme individualism (or reactionary cultural nationalism) are checked in that they fall outside the scope of the accepted norm. Sin, by extension, has to do with the objectification of the body or body collective in such a way as to render its significance relegated to its service as an instrument of another's enjoyment.

Self consciousness is moderated by responsibilities to community (external commitments), without any thought to an eternal self. This is a measured sense of autonomy, it is an autonomous existence in that it is associated with freedom from essentialism (as expressed through sexism, racism, classism, homophobia, and environmental destruction), yet it does not entail a freedom from relationship and the obligations entailed by relationship.[11] The key is individual subjectivity in creative tension with the demand for quality of relationship (community). In contrast, essentialism is the reduction of a group or class of people to a single category or cluster of categories that promotes through law, social arrangements, etc., their subordination and the subordination of their power to define themselves in more wholistic terms.[12] This is most often cast in anti-black terms, yet essentialism can manifest as a pro-black stance, as in the case of the Nation of Islam's appeal to a racial or cultural essence. The latter is also harmful in that, as philosopher Robert Birt notes, "it tends to preserve (however clandestinely or in black face) all the conservative values of the white cultural hierarchy, and sometimes harbor[s] a secret contempt for black people concealed behind a rhetoric of glorification."[13] I am not suggesting a crude anti-essentialism that denies the impact of race on African Americans. It is, to the contrary, a recognition of race, but as only one of the factors affecting subjectivity in the context of the United States.

It must be remembered that essentialist notions of black identity entail not only the "thing-ness" imposed by external oppressors, but also the reification of a certain sense of blackness promoted from within. This would include the various forms of oppression discussed in black theology, but it would also protect the individual's quest for "cultural fulfillment" that concerns Victor Anderson. As Anderson notes, black and womanist theologies have unwittingly enforced forms of essentialism in ways that actually counter the struggle for a liberated existence.[14] Think for example of black theology's early focus on the black male body and its need for liberation against racism. This preoccupation, of necessity, meant little attention to the black female body and the sexism implicitly accepted by black male theologians and the churches they claim to represent. This attention to the more humanistic possibilities serves to better understand the contributions of black churches to this individualism and essentialized sense of being. For example, it should be of interest that the role of churches in fashion and beauty contests of the early and mid-twentieth century and the sense of middle-class individualism inherent takes place during the period in which the church's doctrine turns toward a spiritual individualism and the downplaying of social activism—communal responsibilities.

The insight and warning offered by Hazel Carby, in *Race Men*, should not be forgotten. This Theology of Immanence must maintain an awareness of any tendency to discuss the black body strictly in terms of the black male body. The two are not synonymous.[15] Furthermore, on both fronts, black male and female theologians have often discussed the pleasures of the body strictly in terms of heterosexual orientation and in this way they have buttressed a long history of homophobia (a form of essentialism) within black theology and black churches.[16] The challenge of theology is to continuously question dominant notions of identity and authenticity. I am ever mindful of Stuart Hall's warning that we must understand experience within the context of representation: "It is only through the way in which we represent and imagine ourselves that we come to know how we are constituted and who we are."[17] The importance of cultural criticism for this form of theology is clearly expressed by what it teaches concerning the human body and the ways in which we talk about the body.

If evil and sin are defined as suggested here, liberation, then, has to do with the freedom and 'space' to maintain subjectivity on a variety of levels, to remain visible and engaged. It is the death of black invisibility through a freedom to 'be' in complex ways. And with respect to this, the necessary tension between locations is the equivalent of faith because it requires belief (and action) without complete 'proof' that it is in fact possible to occupy these various locations simultaneously.

Religion, in light of these comments, amounts to the collected stories of struggle for subjectivity and theology is the articulation of these stories.[18] A move away from pre-language ideas of religion and religious experience open it to investigation, even by those who understand themselves as religiously "other." The benefit of this is that it avoids the external vs. internal criticism argument used by many in black theology to discount certain types of criticism. Their argument has traditionally been that the Christ event is the central claim of black theology and only those who "recognize" the centrality of this event can provide an internal critique. A careful read of black theological texts will demonstrate that only internal critiques are responded to in substantial ways.[19]

Some in Black theology will consider my work a form of philosophy of religion, but not theology because it is not "God" talk in traditional terms. Others might argue that it is ideology, not theology. Those who make this argument probably draw from Cone's definition of ideology as "deformed thought, meaning that a certain idea or ideas are nothing but the function of the subjective interest of an individual or group."[20] Following Cone's definition, ideology is non-liberative interpretation, a subjective assertion of self.[21] In opposition to this, for apologetic Black theology, there is the objective truth contained in God's revelation. However, even this attachment to divine revelation does not free liberation theologies from the possibility of being overly subjective. Liberation theologies by nature are somewhat subjective, concerned with a particular perspective and, as a result, are themselves open to the charge of being ideology. Was not that an early critique? In the words of James Cone:

> When people ask me, "How do you know that what you say is true?" my reply is: "Ultimately, I don't know and neither does anybody else." We are creatures of history, not divine beings. I cannot claim infinite knowledge. What I can do is to bear witness to my story, to tell it and live it, as the story grips my life and pulls me out of the nothingness into being. However, I am not imprisoned within my story. Indeed, when I understand truth as story, I am more likely to be open to other people's truth stories. As I listen to other stories, I am invited to move out of the subjectivity of my own story into another realm of thinking and acting.[22]

A humanist theological discourse does not embrace divinely inspired mediation of "truth" implied in this quotation. But, even with that said, there is a sense in which it is monitored. I would argue that the claims and concerns of this proposed discourse are measured and corrected by the demands of community. Life in/between community is not a limitation on the self's quest for meaning, rather it is an extension of that quest; in some respects, it is the culmination of that quest in that it brings into creative tension community and the individual.

The above is my attempt to initiate a conversation concerning the plausibility and dimensions of black humanist studies.[23] What I have said concerning the rough contours of black humanist theological discourse is only a beginning, an invitation for additional thought regarding one particular way of interpreting the movement and development of black America. The depiction of black humanism's nature (and therefore black humanist studies) remains muddy at this time. However, clarity will only come (if it is at all possible) with additional work, and much work is necessary in order for black humanist studies to become a recognizable academic and social project.

Toward Black Humanist Studies Part Two: Pedagogical Considerations[1]

In the previous essay of this section I proposed a humanist way of doing theology and, by necessity, an alternative conceptualization of black religion. While I hope the humanist theology presented serves to ground a mode of black humanist studies that has some influence on the manner in which black religion is studied (and written about) within the Academy, I also recognize that most within the Academy are accountable for more than publications. Scholars are also teachers responsible for sharing information with students—some eager and others less energetic.[2] It is apparent, then, I should not conclude this text without giving some attention to pedagogical ramifications of my proposed turn toward black humanist studies. That is, how does one conceive of the classroom and one's role in it based on the sensibilities of black humanist studies, and the emphasis on transformed consciousness and the human body entailed by black humanist principles?

Unpacking the Educational Process

I would like to begin addressing this question through a reconceptualization of the space in which education takes place. To do so, I suggest we think about education as a ritual moment or process comprising a variety of realities and materials that at its best challenges, and at times transforms consciousness on the individual and collective levels.[3] Understanding that the educational process is triadic in nature—composed of body, building, community—my intention is to give attention to physicality (and aesthetics) as a way of rethinking the classroom transference of information. Brief consideration to the body in the classroom as a pedagogical force is my chosen mode of approach to this discussion. This entails also a movement from banking models of education to strategies that maintain an awareness of the importance of non-text based materials.

The body becomes important because of the way in which it displays meaning and value through clothing, gestures, habits, mannerisms, postures, or objects associated with it. Attention to the body is also important because the classroom understood as ritualized space suggests that there be an importance given to the sensory meaning of actions and words, which are experienced and expressed through physicality. The body is not incidental and the nondiscursive ways of knowing, hence, should not be downplayed nor denied because, as William Doty notes, "the human body is itself an important means of communicating. Its postures, its inborn responses to stimuli, its moods and beauties, its positions in social intercourse: all these may be used in the communicative process. . . ."[4] The body is important because it is an intersubjective reality and "its actions often communicate meaning and, therefore, present an interpretive problem. We not only speak English, we move and pose in English. . . . The body is in important respects text-like in its readability, and interpreting its communication is at least as complex as translating from Sanskirt to Japanese."[5] Ronald Grimes, one of the founding scholars of Ritual Studies, also pushes for an understanding of the body as of primary importance, as more than just a footnote or affirmation of verbal exchange. Rather "symbolic actions carry in their levels of complexity, but they have in common that they are sometimes channels of communication. Our bodily actions are not mere punctuation marks for verbal ones. Rather, they function as a 'second language' articulated simultaneously alongside our words. Words are not necessarily primary."[6] And gestures are metaphors of the body.[7] Much of my emphasis has entailed the importance of the body as a multivalent reality; why would not the implications of this assertion also affect teaching philosophy?

The Body's Pedagogical Significance

As I have noted elsewhere, the shape, makeup, and appearance of bodies within the classroom have changed over the years, moving from a space of sameness to a marked space of difference (some difference anyway). And the presence of these new bodies points to societal, political, and other changes—signs of which are often borne in the bodies. As Franz Fanon and Hortense Spiller have argued, the body is a site of memory and meaning that, through its markings, speaks concretely of racial, political, and social dynamics. It is, to quote Ronald Grimes, "both 'thou' and 'it'—at once a distinctive, animate, socially aware subject and an object painted, broken, adored, abused, and examined. As a function of the body's intersubjectivity, its actions often communicate meaning. . . ."[8] The presence of these differing bodies has perhaps resulted in new attention to the significance of the body's presence that could no longer be taken for granted. Education informed by these sensitivities is enhanced in that the forms of exchange are broadened to include the physical presence of those involved. In this way, "successful" education is forced to include an understanding and appreciation of the bodies involved in ways that move bodily representation away from oppressive—status quo—positioning. The teaching moment moves away from a strict appreciation for the mind and ideas and connects these realities to the physical presence and meaning of the bodies gathered in the space of learning. Because of this, teachers come to recognize that pedagogical issues must take into consideration not only curricular concerns, but must also understand that the learning experience is shaped by the "space" in which learning takes place. Education comes to involve individual and group actualization.[9] In this way, the body becomes an important means of basic data related to the body-cultural existence. The teaching moment moves away from a traditional mind/body split.

Education and Ritual Process

Furthermore, through this shift, a concern with mutual exchange takes on greater importance. Both those who teach and those who learn are affected by the teaching process because in real ways they are the same: teachers learn and learners teach. Attention to the body also highlights the expression of beliefs and ideas beyond written textual forms. Related to the subject matter of this book, it forces an understanding of religion as intimately connected to concrete settings, housed in concrete forms. It allows us to hold in creative tension the material and nonmaterial concerns of religion. This is simply to suggest that physicality is important in the classroom setting and attention to this may enhance the learning process. This, then, requires a change in resources used in the classroom—a broadened range of materials and nonmaterials. This refocusing should enliven and add complexity to our discussion of religiosity and religious reality.

Perhaps, for example, a course on black religion should include study of doctrine and dance, institutional structures and decorative culture—as well as theistic and nontheistic traditions. And perhaps we should make use of the written text and also opportunities for students to experience, through their bodies, black religion.

To undertake such an approach, we might begin by understanding places of learning as ritualized space in which learning takes place because of exchange entailing not only written materials, but nonwritten texts such as the body. In fact, such a shift to a larger array of forms of meaning making outside the written text is required by sensitivity to the body and other modes of expression. One, of course, cannot afford to dismiss the written word; it is too much a part of the societies in which we live. Yet, the record of our consciousness is not limited to such texts. What is required involves something along the lines of historian of religions Lawrence Sullivan's call for the end of the text. This is a call similar to the "death" of this or that idea or ideology by means of which is suggested a recognition of the limits of the written word for producing, describing, and interpreting our historical consciousness.[10]

Ritual Studies and Ronald Grimes in particular are important to this shift because of their premise that the verbal and written materials are not the primary means by which to understand the significance of a ritual activity, understanding nonverbal elements such as choreography.[11] In the words of Grimes, "Rituals 'transpire,' they breathe and fluctuate; they are performed in 'animations,' soul givings. And they do so in human bodies who perform them, who become ensouled in ritual acts." Furthermore, according to Doty, "a ritual, as a formal social action, is an event that utilizes aural and kinetic patterns to express or communicate shared values and to inculcate or elicit them. It is more sensuously immediate than most myths, except as myths are actualized in performance contexts."[12] Through this move to Ritual Studies, one has an opportunity to turn attention typically given to the body and other materials—such as clothing and pictures—toward the implication of these materials for practice, or education. These materials become, in this way, a primary symbol for larger meanings. That is to say, students come to recognize that black religion does not always entail discussion of God or gods, but rather it can also center on "earthbound" materials and sensibilities. As Lawrence Sullivan urges, "religious studies could look not only at dreams but at shadows, at flowers, at sounds, at pottery as symbolic vehicles for the full load of human experience. . . . as teachers of religious studies, such alternative significant realities are available to us in abundant supply and, as cultural resources, we should make clear their power, logic, and coherence to our students."[13] The body becomes a symbolic vehicle for religious experience as it is discussed in the classroom. There is something ritualistic about this process.

Rituals are communicative processes by which persons find meaning and meaningful systems of symbols that relate to and often critique social realities. In this way, the ritualized space of learning has something to say concerning notions of justice and liberation. It becomes the nexus between worlds of culture in which liminal realities collide in a creative manner, resulting in alterations that enhance our ability to understand and shape our environments.

Such a depiction of the educational process is certainly in keeping with the perspective of Mary Douglas. Readers may recall that Douglas argues for an understanding of the human body as an image of the larger social reality, the social system. Tied to this, and of most importance for our purposes, is her assertion that religious symbols and tools—in this case the pedagogical significance of the body—also influences and structures social arrangements. Therefore, education as conceived here allows for a "continuous transformation" of the individual within community.[14]

The Educational and Masking

When the body is given this sort of consideration and importance within our pedagogical structures, it is useful to also discuss the various ways in which the body is presented. I will limit my discussion to a brief mention of "masking."

This process of concealment involves a transformation meant to project the person as something "other" than the self, to attempt concealment of identity.[15] Within the classroom this might be understood as an attempt to enter ritualized space and approach theological issues in an objective manner—to "don" anonymity. This issue of masking, to use Ronald Grimes' terminology, often surfaces with respect to questions such as: how much of one's own faith stance ought to be shared with students in the classroom, and what is the purpose of this sharing? Masking, in this respect, can allow the wearer to stand outside the circle, so to speak, and in this way control the action without personally risking anything. Nothing is risked because the person masked (teacher or student) gains, through pretense, the authority and voice of the dead—Hegel, Kant, DuBois, and others, thereby securing a measure of social control. It can involve an act of bad faith by allow-ing the wearer to avoid carrying the weight of his or her history and the existential and ontological consequences of this history. Yet, this is not to say that all masking is necessarily "bad." Some masking may be unavoidable if not useful, and it is difficult at best to dissect the various modes of masking. In one sense, masking can help individuals develop a sensitivity to the socio-cultural context of another, which may, in turn, promote dialogue.

In the final analysis, understanding the body's role in the develop-ment and expression of meaning may allow for a more critical evalua-tion of the self, community, and religious traditions in the classroom by giving attention to a fuller range of meaning making processes and content. Through a recognition of the body's significance, the teaching and research of black religion is better equipped to explain what it means to be black and religious, with style and depth.

Notes

Preface

1. This chapter is a greatly expanded essay based on "Against the Grain: The Question for this Black, Atheist Theologian Is Why?" *Free Inquiry*, Volume 21, No. 1 (Winter 2000/01): 49–50.

Introduction

1. Edith Hamilton, *Mythology: Timeless Tales of Gods and Heroes* (New York: New American Library, 1969), 69.
2. Hubert Harrison, "On a Certain Conservatism in Negroes," in *The Negro and the Nation* (New York: Cosmo-Advocate Publishing Co., 1917), 41, 42.
3. See Stephen R. Haynes's *Noah's Curse: The Biblical Justification of American Slavery* (New York: Oxford University Press, 2002).
4. Genesis 11: 4–6 (King James Version).
5. Haynes, *Noah's Curse*, 43.
6. Ibid., 46.
7. Ibid., 47.
8. Ibid., 51.
9. Ibid., 61.
10. This project extends beyond my previous work in that it addresses more than just the historical development of humanism. This project is also concerned with humanism as a hermeneutic and praxis. In other work, at best, I have framed the possibility of humanism as a praxis. It is only here that I give attention to how it might actually work in this capacity.
11. Atheistic humanism dominants the discussion of African American humanism in this book because it provides the best contrast between traditionally religious modalities of life orientation and humanism. Other humanist frameworks overlap with, for example, prophetic Christianity in ways that prevent a clear understanding of what humanism offers as a unique orientation.

Chapter One

1. This essay reframes arguments found in: Anthony B. Pinn, "Anybody There?: Reflections on African American Humanism," *Religious Humanism*, Volume XXXI,

Nos. 3 and 4 (Summer/Fall: 1997): 61–78 and "Introduction," *By These Hands: A Documentary History of African American Humanism* (New York: New York University Press, 2001). It draws more heavily from Anthony B. Pinn, *Varieties of African American Religious Experience* (Minneapolis: Fortress Press, 1998), 157–167.

2. Corliss Lamont, *The Philosophy of Humanism* (New York: Frederick Ungar Publishing, Co., 1965), 17–18.

3. See Henry F. May, *The Enlightenment in America* (New York: Oxford University Press, 1976).

4. John H. Dietrich, "Unitarianism and Humanism," in *What If The World Went Humanist?: Ten Sermons*, selected by Mason Olds (Yellow Springs, OH: Fellowship of Religious Humanists, 1989), 58.

5. Ibid., 63. The reader will likely find the other sermons in this volume interesting particularly, in light of the focus of this chapter, the following sermons: "What If The World Went Humanist?" and "Religion and Morality."

6. Meyer, "Secular Transcendence," 531.

7. See: *Humanist Manifestoes I and II* (Buffalo, NY: Prometheus, 1973).

8. Lamont, *The Philosophy of Humanism*, 24, 25.

9. Ibid., 52.

10. In Mason Olds, "What Is Religious Humanism?" *Free Inquiry*, Volume 16, No. 4 (Fall 1996): 13.

11. Although I find Benjamin Mays' comments useful in the post-1920s section, his comment concerning the period prior to 1914 is incorrect. He writes: "It is significant to note that prior to 1914, one finds no ideas of god that imply doubt and repudiation" (Benjamin E. Mays, *The Negro's God as Reflected in His Literature* [New York: Atheneum, 1973], 244). The information I provide in this section refutes his claim. Also see: Lawrence Levine's work and Sterling Brown's writings, and V. P. Franklin, *Black Self-Determination: A Cultural History of the Faith of the Fathers* (Westport, CT: Lawrence Hill and Co., 1984), the section on "Slave Theology and Morality" beginning on 51. Much of this early humanism is found in blues and work songs. For a discussion of this, see: Anthony B. Pinn, *Why, Lord?: Suffering and Evil in Black Theology* (New York: Continuum, 1995), chapters 5–6.

12. Daniel Alexander Payne, "Daniel Payne's Protestation of Slavery," *Lutheran Herald and Journal of the Franckean Synod* (August 1, 1839): 114–115.

13. I have discussed at some length the humanist implications of the blues and folk wisdom elsewhere and will not repeat that information here. Those interested in that discussion should refer to Pinn, *Why, Lord?*, chapter 5.

14. Arthur Fauset, *Black Gods of the Metropolis: Negro Religious Cults of the Urban North* (Philadelphia: University of Pennsylvania Press, 1944), 7.

15. Roy D. Morrison, II, "The Emergence of Black Theology in America," *The A.M.E. Zion Quarterly Review*, Volume XCIV, No. 3 (October 1982): 6.

16. James Baldwin, *The Fire Next Time* (New York: Dell Books, 1962), 42.

17. Ibid., 43–44.

18. Ibid., 46.

19. Ibid., 47.

20. Ibid., 56–57. Also see pages 64–67.

21. Ibid., 97.

22. Eugene Levy, *James Weldon Johnson: Black Leader, Black Voice* (Chicago: The University of Chicago Press), 15.

23. Ibid., 19.

24. J. Saunders Redding, edited with an Introduction by Faith Berry, *A Scholar's Conscience: Selected Writings of J. Saunders Redding, 1942–1977* (Louisville: The University Press of Kentucky, 1992).

25. Redding, "From On Being Negro in America," in *A Scholar's Conscience*, 49.

26. Ibid.

27. Ibid., 52.

28. Ibid., 52.

29. Ibid., 52.

30. Ibid., 53–54.

31. Ibid., 53.

32. Trudier Harris, "Three Black Women Writers and Humanism: A Folk Perspective," in R. Baxter Miller, ed., *African-American Literature and Humanism* (Lexington, KY: University Press of Kentucky), 54.

33. Ibid., 72.

34. Alice Walker, "the only reason you want to go to heaven is that you have been driven out of your mind (off your land and out of your lover's arms): clear seeing inherited religion and reclaiming the pagan self," *On The Issues*, Vol. VI, No. 2 (Spring 1997): 19.

35. Ibid., 19–20.

36. Italics added, ibid., 23. See Alice Walker's *The Color Purple* for another discussion of theology and the problem of evil. The conversations between Shug and Celie are telling.

Chapter Two

1. This essay draws ideas, wording, and some of its conceptual framework from Anthony B. Pinn, "Anybody There?: Reflections on African American Humanism, *Religious Humanism*, Volume XXXI, Nos. 3 and 4 (Summer/Fall: 1997): 67–74. It relies more heavily on Anthony B. Pinn, *Varieties of African American Religious Experience* (Minneapolis: Fortress Press, 1998), 167–183.

2. Mays, *The Negro's God*, 243.

3. Langston Hughes, *Good Morning Revolution: Uncollected Writings of Social Protest by Langston Hughes*, Introduction by Faith Berry (New York: Carol Publishing Group), xvi–xvii.

4. Robin D. G. Kelley, "Comrades, Praise Gawd for Lenin and Them!: Ideology and Culture Among Black Communities in Alabama, 1930–1935," *Science and Society*, Volume 52, No. 1 (Spring 1988), 61–62. Also see Robin Kelley's " Afric's Sons with Banners Red, " in *Imagining Home: Class, Culture, and Nationalism in the African Diaspora* (New York: Verso, 1994).

5. Ibid., 64.

6. Ibid., 65–66.

7. Nell Irvin Painter, *The Narrative of Hosea Hudson: His Life as a Negro Communist in the South* (Cambridge, MA: Harvard University Press, 1979), 133–134.

8. Ibid.
9. Ibid., 134–135. Others who meshed humanism with political involvement include A. Philip Randolph, T. Thomas Fortune, and Paul Robeson. The nontheistic leanings of the latter come across indirectly in the following statement made by Harold Cruse concerning Robeson's romanitization of the "negro worker":

> . . . Robeson and [his] middle-class-leftwing ethos truly idealized . . . . nice, upright Negro workers; who, *even if they did go to church and worship God and not Russia*, at least tilled the Southern soil as solid citizen sharecroppers. . . ."

(Harold Cruse, "Jews and Negroes in the Communist Party," in *The Crisis of the Negro Intellectual: A Historical Analysis of the Failure of Black Leadership* (New York: William Morrow and Company/Quill, 1967, 1984), 236.

10. Ibid., 147.
11. Rev. J. M. Lawson, Jrs., "Statement of Purpose," *The Student Voice*, Volume 1, No. 1 (June 1960), in Clayborne Caron, senior editor, *The Student Voice, 1960–1965: Periodical of the Student Nonviolent Coordinating Committee* (Westport, CT: Meckler, 1990), 2.
12. Stokley Carmichael and Charles Hamilton, *Black Power* (New York: Vintage Books, 1967) quoted in Norman Harris, *Connecting Times: The Sixties in Afro-American Fiction* (Jackson, MS: University Press of Mississippi, 1988), 91.
13. James Forman, "Corrupt Black preachers," in *The Making of Black Revolutionaries* (Washington, DC: Open Hand Publishing, Inc., 1985), 58.
14. Forman, "God Is Dead: A Question of Power," in *Black Revolutionaries*, 80–81.
15. Ibid., 83.
16. Seale, *Sieze the time*, "Introduction," 3.
17. Huey P. Newton, in Toni Morrison, ed., *To Die For The People: The Writings of Huey P. Newton* (New York: Writers and Readers Publishing, Inc., 1995), 63–64.
18. Ibid., 64.
19. Eldridge Cleaver, "On Becoming," Four Vignettes found in *Soul On Ice* (New York: McGraw-Hill, 1967), 4–5.
20. Eldridge Cleaver, " 'The Christ' and His Teachings," in Four Vignettes found in *Soul On Ice*, 34.
21. Seale, *Sieze the Time*, 429.
22. Mark D. Morrison-Reed, *Black Pioneers in a White Denomination*, 3rd edition (Boston: Skinner House Books, 1994), xii. For additional information on the Unitarian Universalist Association in Harlem see: Juan Floyd-Thomas, *Creating a Temple and a Forum: Religion, Culture, and Politics in the Harlem Unitarian Church, 1920–1956* (University of Pennsylvania Dissertation, 2000).
23. Ibid., 91.
24. Ibid., 92.
25. Quoted in ibid., 94.
26. Ibid., 95.
27. Morrison-Reed, *Black Pioneers*, 120.
28. Ibid., 132–133.
29. Quoted in ibid., 135.

30. Unitarian Universalist Commission on Appraisal to the General Assembly, *Empowerment: One Denomination's Quest for Racial Justice, 1967–1982* (Boston: Unitarian Universalist Association, 1983), 24.
31. Interview with Norm Allen, Jr., January 1997, in Amherst, New York.
32. "An African-American Humanist Declaration," *Free Inquiry*, Volume 10, No. 2 (Spring 1990): 13.
33. Ibid., 14–15.

Chapter Three

1. This essay is drawn from the following: Anthony B. Pinn, "Of Works and Faith: The New Religious Right and Humanist Ethics," *Religious Humanism*, Volume XXXIV, Nos. 3 and 4 (Summer/Fall 2000): 41–54.
2. In chapter four I make a transition with respect to terminology and refer to this movement as the Christian Right for the sake of increased clarity.

    Some may argue that this section—chapters three and four—is wrongheaded because humanism and fundamentalism are antithetical. This is precisely the point. Because of the radical distinction between fundamentalism and humanism, a humanist critique of the former presents in a very clear way the nature and meaning of humanist principles. The radical opposition highlights the principles I am interested in bringing to the attention of readers. If, however, I were interested in a discussion of plausible conversation partners for black humanism I would include a chapter on liberal theologians. Nonetheless, my concern is not with conversation partners but with the function of humanist principles and this is best explicated through opposition.
3. See: Steve Bruce, "The Moral Majority: The politics of Fundamentalism in Secular Society," in Lionel Caplan, ed., *Studies in Religious Fundamentalism* (Albany: State University of New York Press, 1987), 177–181.
4. Stephen D. Johnson and Joseph B. Tamney, ed., *The Political Role of Religion in the United States* (Boulder, CO: Westview Press, 1986), 146–148.
5. Bruce B. Lawrence, *Defenders of God: The Fundamentalist Revolt Against the Modern Age* (Columbia: University of South Carolina Press, 1989), 27.
6. Stephen D. Johnson and Joseph B. Tamney, ed., *The Political Role of Religion in the United States* (Boulder, CO: Westview Press Inc., 1986), 152. Also see: Walter H. Capps, *The New Religious Right: Piety, Patriotism, and Politics* (Columbia: University of South Carolina, 1990), 14–15.
7. Samuel S. Hill and Dennis E. Owen, *The New Religious/Political Right in America* (Nashville: Abingdon, 1982), 16–17.
8. Ibid., 151–152.
9. Corliss Lamont, *The Philosophy of Humanism* (New York: Philosophical Library, 1949); William Ernest Henley, "Invictus."
10. Lamont, *Humanism as a Philosophy*, 19–21.
11. I discuss five principles as the foundation for black humanism, while Lamont speaks in terms of eight general principles. This difference does not constitute a contraction in that many of Lamont's principles are captured in a condensed form in the principles I suggest. Furthermore, it should be noted that these principles,

although somewhat unified and embraced by most humanists, are not connected to one homogeneous system rightfully known as humanism. There are various forms of humanism, including agnostic humanism and religious humanism. One could easily add to this list freethinkers (who reject religious revelation and the authority of the Church) rationalists (for whom reason and verifiability through experience are supreme), members of Ethical Culture societies (who are dedicated to the "right"), advocates of "dialectical materialism" (premised upon the work of Karl Marx), scientific humanism, democratic humanism, skepticism, and deism. Even with these additions, the list may not be complete.

12. *Humanist Manifestos I and II* (Buffalo, NY: Prometheus Books, 1973).
13. Ibid., 7.
14. Ibid., 17. Two of the signers of the second manifesto are African Americans— A. Philip Randolph and James Farmer.
15. Ibid., 15.
16. Ibid., 23.
17. Kurtz, *Forbidden Fruit*, 17.
18. Although Kurtz's work places strong emphasis on agnostic, atheistic and skeptic forms of humanism—with their strong critic of traditional forms of theism—he, as did Lamont and the signers of both manifestos, acknowledges that there are basic elements of a humanistic system of ethics embraced by all humanist camps. The various categories of humanism mentioned throughout this essay are distinctive due to the emphasis given to particular humanist principles as opposed to more intrinsic differences. Within each of these camps is a recognition that human purpose and meaning are developed and articulated only in respect to the needs, interests, and experiences of living species.
19. Jean-Paul Sartre, *Existentialism and Human Emotions* (New York: Carol Publishing Group, 1957, 1990), 51.

Chapter Four

1. First presented at All Souls Unitarian Universalist Church, Kansas City, Missouri as "When This Life On Earth Is Just Practice: Thoughts on the Christian Right's Motivations and Preoccupations."
2. George M. Marsden, *Understanding Fundamentalism and Evangelicalism* (Grand Rapids, MI: William B. Eerdmans Publishing Company, 1991), 91.
3. See: Steve Bruce, "The Moral Majority: The Politics of Fundamentalism in Secular Society," in Lionel Caplan, ed., *Studies in Religious Fundamentalism* (Albany: State University of New York Press, 1987), 177–181; George M. Marsden, *Understanding Fundamentalism and Evangelicalism* (Grand Rapids, MI: William B. Eerdmans Publishing Company, 1991), note 1, page 1.
4. Ibid., 94.
5. Stephen D. Johnson and Joseph B. Tamney, ed., *The Political Role of Religion in the United States* (Boulder, CO: Westview Press, 1986), 146, 148.
6. Quoted in Susan Friend Harding, *The Book of Jerry Falwell: Fundamentalist Language and Politics* (Princeton: Princeton University Press, 2000), 22. One

should not assume this push for political involvement entailed a unified evangelical front. While most evangelicals held liberalism suspect, not all channeled this into involvement in what is commonly referred to as the Religious Right or more precisely the complex and diverse Christian Right. Concerning the make-up of the Christian Right, it is safe to say that its members are evangelical but not all evangelicals are in the Christian Right.

7. Ibid., 156.
8. Walter H. Capps, *The New Religious Right: Piety, Patriotism, and Politics* (Columbia: University of South Carolina, 1990), 6.
9. Cited in Steve Bruce, "The Inevitable Failure of the New Christian Right," in Steve Bruce et al., eds., *The Rapture of Politics: The Christian Right as the United States Approaches the Year 2000* (New Brunswick, NJ: Transaction Publishers, 1995), 8.
10. Ibid., 9.
11. Ibid.
12. Steve Bruce, "The Inevitable Failure of the New Christian Right," in Steve Bruce et al., eds., *The Rapture of Politics: The Christian Right as the United States Approaches the Year* 2000 (New Brunswick, NJ: Transaction Publishers, 1995), 10–11.
13. Ibid., 12–13.
14. Ibid., 24–25.
15. Walter H. Capps, *The New Religious Right: Piety, Patriotism, and Politics* (Columbia: University of South Carolina, 1990), 186.
16. Jerry Falwell, *Listen, America!* (Garden City, NY: Doubleday and Company, 1980). Cited in Michael Lienesch, *Redeeming America: Piety & Politics in the New Christian Right* (Chapel Hill: The University of North Carolina Press, 1993), 224.
17. Susan Friend Harding, *The Book of Jerry Falwell: Fundamentalist Language and Politics* (Princeton: Princeton University Press, 2000), 230.
18. George M. Marsden, *Understanding Fundamentalism and Evangelicalism* (Grand Rapids, MI: William B. Eerdmans Publishing Company, 1991), 112.
19. Harding, *The Book of Jerry Falwell,* 241.
20. Quoted in ibid., 242.
21. Ibid., 244.
22. Cited in Michael Lienesch, *Redeeming America: Piety & Politics in the New Christian Right* (Chapel Hill: The University of North Carolina Press, 1993), 228.
23. Lienesch, *Redeeming America,* 23.
24. John Bunyan, *The Pilgrim's Progress* (New York: Penguin Books [1965] 1987), 13.
25. It goes without saying that Christianity is not the only tradition that contains some notion of an afterlife. However, for the context of the United States, it is an obvious place to begin such a discussion. Furthermore, heaven and the afterlife are combined in this article because they tend to function in an overlapping way; the former without the latter is illogical.
26. See, e.g., St. Augustine's *The Confessions* and *City of God.* Peter Brown's *Augustine of Hippo: A Biography* (Berkeley: University of California Press, 1967) remains one of the best treatments of St. Augustine available.
27. Brown, *Augustine of Hippo,* 159.
28. St. Augustine, *City of God,* Book XXII, an abridged, Version from the translation by Gerald G. Walsh, Demetrius B. Zema, Grace Monahan, and Daniel J. Honan (Garden City, NY: Image Books, 1958), 544–45.

29. Before moving on, it must be noted that my general statements concerning Christian notions of the afterlife and heaven (and hell) do not apply to all Christians. I would not want to falsely stereotype Christians. However, for the sake of argument, my themes are useful as long as my disclaimer is remembered.

30. See, e.g. Richard Wright's *The Outsider* (New York: Harper, 1953). Also see Albert Camus' *The Plague*. These two texts are good examples of the existentialist dilemma. Those interested in additional materials such also see the work of Frantz Fanon and Jean-Paul Satre, among others.

31. Floyd W. Hayes, III, "Fanon, Oppression, and Resentment: The Black Experience in the United States," in Lewis R. Gordon, T. Dean Sharpley Whiting, and Renée T. White, ed., *Fanon: A Critical Reader* (Cambridge, MA: Blackwell Publishers, 1996), 15.

32. Richard Wright, *Black Boy* (New York: Harper & Row, Publishers, 1966), 281.

33. I think the current trend back to religious organizations such as Christian churches speaks to this desire for certainty and order in an alienated and decentered world.

Chapter Five

1. A longer version of this essay was published as "Handling My Business: Rap Music's Humanist Sensibilities," in Anthony B. Pinn, ed., *Noise and Spirit: Rap Music's Religious and Spiritual Sensibilities* (New York: New York University Press, 2003).

2. Gerald H. Hinkle, *Art as Event: An Aesthetic for the Performing Arts* (Washington, DC: University Press of America, Inc., 1979), 6.

3. Michael Gardiner, "Bakhtin and the Metaphorics of Perception," in Ian Heywood and Barry Sandywell, eds., *Interpreting Visual Culture: Explorations in the Hermeneutics of the Visual* (New York: Routledge, 1999), 59.

4. Bernard Schwarze, "Religion, Rock, and Research," in *Sacred Music of the Secular City: From Blues to Rap*, a special issue of *Black Sacred Music: A Journal of Theomusicology*, Volume 6, No. 1 (Spring 1992): 85.

5. Clive Marsh's review of *Good Taste, Bad Taste, and Christian Taste: Aesthetics in Religious Life* by Frank Burch Brown, *Reviews in Religion and Theology*, Volume 8, Issue 5 (November 2001): 533.

6. It would be unreasonable to argue that humanism dominates rap music as it would be completely false to suggest that humanism is numerically significant (to the extent levels of participation can be assessed) in the context of the United States. However, it is present, and the viability and importance of humanism in black communities in general and rap music in particular should not be measured strictly in terms of numerical representation. It is more fruitful to give attention to the strength of the arguments and orientations present than to simply reduce significance to levels of membership.

7. Much of the information for this portion of the argument is drawn from a larger work, the Edward Cadbury Lectures delivered at the University of Birmingham (UK), February 2002.

8. ScarFace, "Dairy of a Madman," *Mr. ScarFace is Back*.

9. Robert Birt, "Existence, Identity, and Liberation," in Lewis Gordon, ed., *Existence in Black: An Anthology of Black Existential Philosophy* (New York: Routledge, 1997), 206.

10. Ibid., 211.

11. Mark LeVine, "KRS-One: Hip-hop Clergy." Beliefnet Celebrity Interviews and Profiles. <www.beliefnet.com>.

12. William R. Jones, *Is God a White Racist?: A Preamble to Black Theology* (Boston: Beacon Press, 1999).

13. KRS-One, "Take It to God," *Spiritual Minded.*

14. <http://www.patricdaily.f9.co.uk.DOGGYS.htm>

15. "KRS-One and the Temple of Hiphop," found at: <http:/www.gospelcity.com/interviews/0202/krs-one_2.hph>

16. Ibid.

17. Queen Latifah (with Karen Hunter), *Ladies First: Revelations of a Strong Woman* (New York: William Morrow and Company, Inc., 1999), 173.

18. Queen Latifah, "Ladies First," *All Hail The Queen.*

19. James Plath interview with Koko Taylor, "Queen of the Blues: Koko Taylor Talks about Her Subjects," *Clockwatch Review: A Journal of the Arts,* Volume 9, No. 1–2 (1994–1995): 117–131. Found at: <http://titan.iqu.edu/~jplath/ taylor.html>

20. Alice Walker, *In Search of Our Mothers' Gardens: Womanist Prose* (New York: Harvest/Harcourt Brace Jovanovich, Publishers, 1983), 37.

21. Ibid.

22. Queen Latifah, *Ladies First,* 19.

23. Queen Latifah, "U.N.I.T.Y.," *Black Reign.*

24. From The Color Purple. Cited in Alice Walker, "The Only Reason You Want To Go To Heaven Is That You Have Been Driven Out Of Your Mind," reprinted in Anthony B. Pinn, ed., *By These Hands: A Documentary History of African American Humanism* (New York: New York University Press, 2001), 289.

25. Ibid., 290.

26. See: "Latifah's Law," *All Hail the Queen.*

27. Queen Latifah, *Ladies First* 109.

28. Ibid., 290.

29. Walker, "The Only Reason You Want To Go To Heaven," 296.

30. Readers should keep in mind that many black humanists reject the God concept, but this is not a prerequisite for an embrace of black humanism.

31. Arrested Development, "Fishin 4 Religion," in *3 Years, 5 Months & 2 days in the Life of . . .* (New York: Chrysalis Records, Inc., 1992).

32. Ibid.

33. ScarFace, "Mind Playin' Tricks 94," *The Diary* (Beverly Hills, CA: Noo Trybe Records, 1994).

34. Ibid.

35. Ibid.

36. Shakur, "Blasphemy," *The Don Killuminati.*

37. Malcolm Venable, "Missing You," *Vibe Magazine* (March 2000), 99.

38. As the following discussion will make clear, I have in mind Albert Camus' *The Rebel,* and in terms of Rene Girard I have in mind *Violence and the Sacred*

[translated by Patrick Gregory (Baltimore: The Johns Hopkins University Press, 1977)]. With respect to Cross Damon, see: Richard Wright's *The Outsider.*

39. Shakur, "Hail Mary," *The Don Killuminati.*
40. While I apply a rather loose and limited interpretation of Camus here. Readers may be interested in analyzing the lyrics of "Hail Mary" and "Blasphemy" in light of, for example, "The Sons of Cain" and "Rebellion and Art" in Camus' *The Rebel* [translated by Anthony Bower (New York: Vintage International, 1991), 26–35, 253–277].
41. Albert Camus, *The Rebel: An Essay on Man in Revolt* (New York: Vintage International, 1991), 20.
42. Herbert Read, "Foreword," in Albert Camus, *The Rebel: An Essay on Man in Revolt* (New York: Vintage International, 1991), vii.
43. Ibid.
44. Shakur, "Black Jesus," *Still I Rise.*
45. Rob Marriott, interview with Tupac Shakur, "Last Testament," in *Vibe Magazine* (November 1996), T7.
46. Ibid.
47. Michael Eric Dyson, *Holler If You Hear Me: Searching for Tupac Shakur* (New York: Basic Civitas Books, 2001), 230.
48. Camus, *The Rebel*, 10.
49. Ibid., 21.
50. Dyson, *Holler*, 208.
51. Jamie Boulding, "Interview with Sage Francis (August 2001): <http://www.hiphopinfinity.com/Articles/SageFrancis_Interview3>.

Chapter Six

1. This essay was presented as part of the Humanist Institute, 2002.
2. Some might find it difficult to initially see the logical coherence of this chapter to the overall work of this volume. Here I provide a final example of how humanist principles—particularly the humanist emphasis on accountability and the historical "weight" of the human body—serve to frame a hermeneutic, a way of interpreting and reading "texts" and events. I believe this exercise, begun in chapter five, is important and a natural component to the volume's agenda in that it provides a sense of an important dimension of humanism's function within black America. As opposed to simply thinking in terms of institutions and practices, this chapter, as did chapter five, demonstrates one way in which black humanists might use their principles, as black Christians use Christian principles, to interpret the world.
3. Readers will note that I make use of the following terms to describe the same group of people: blacks, African Americans, and black Americans. I have no preference for one of these terms over the others, and I believe within any given context one term might be more insightful than another.
4. Frantz Fanon, *Black Skin, White Masks* (New York: Grove Press Inc., 1967), 60.
5. Ibid., 34.
6. Concerning this point, Mary Douglas provides a helpful anthropological discussion of the body and its meaning. See: Mary Douglas, *Natural Symbols: Explorations in Cosmology* (New York: Routledge, 1996).

7. See Charles Long, *Significations* (Minneapolis: Fortress Press, 1986), chapter seven.
8. Michel Foucault, *Discipline and Punish: The Birth of the Prison* (New York: Vintage Books, 1979), 25–26.
9. Quoted in Kenneth Meeks, *Driving While Black* (New York: Broadway Books, 2000), 5.
10. Ira Berlin et al., *Remembering Slavery: African Americans Talk About Their Personal Experiences of Slavery and Freedom* (New York: The New Press/Washington, D.C.: Library of Congress, 1998), 54–55.
11. David A. Harris, *Profiles in Injustice: Why Racial Profiling Cannot Work* (New York: The New Press, 2002), 104.
12. Meeks, *Driving While Black,* 19.
13. Ibid., 26, 34.
14. Harris, *Profiles in Injustice,* 13.
15. Fanon, *Black Skin, White Masks,* 116.

Chapter Seven

1. Sex(uality) entails a recognition that there is a complex and thick interaction between the various modalities of relationship that mark human existence. Some are sex based, others involve sexuality and are not fully captured through attention to libido drive-based interactions.
2. I understand sex(uality) as the term denoting that which extends "beyond our physicality to encompass all of the ways in which the physical is rendered meaningful." ("Introduction," in Stephen Ellingson and M. Christian Green, eds., *Religion and Sexuality in Cross-Cultural Perspective* (New York: Routledge, 2002, 2.) As defined here sex(uality) includes the physical act of love making and the pleasure involved, but it is not limited to this. The erotic, drawing from Paul Tillich's work, in this essay involves an even fuller range of relationships and interactions that are only partially covered through libido desires and needs.
3. Peter Gardella, *Innocent Ecstasy: How Christianity Gave America an Ethic of Sexual Pleasure* (New York: Oxford University Press, 1985), 57.
4. Such developments prior to the Modern Period were given theological power over bodies when, for example, one notes that Aquinas considered sexual desire dangerous to both one's spiritual development and one's physical body. This is not to say that sexual desire was by its very nature problematic. If this were the case even sexual activity between spouses would be sinful. Rather than this, sexual desire was considered an interruption of one's energy and commitment to higher concerns and reason. Albeit mystics countered the preoccupation with reason theologically pushed by scholars such as Aquinas; their efforts to demonstrate the possibility of knowing God through (rather than in spite of) the body did not serve to foster a more general appreciation for the body and the sexual self. There remained a Cartesian privileging of the spirit over the body and its desire/needs. See Meery E. Wiesner-Hauls, *Christianity and Sexuality in the Early Modern World: Regulating Desire, Reforming Practice* (New York: Routledge, 2000), 43–44.
5. Ibid., *Early Modern World: Regulating Desire, Reforming Practice,* 2, 3, 5, 6.

6. Ibid., 9.
7. "Introduction," in Pat Caplan, ed., *The Cultural Construction of Sexuality* (New York: Tavistock Publications, 1987), 7.
8. M. Shawn Copeland, "Body, Representation, and Black Religious Discourse," in John D'Emilio and Estelle B. Freedman, *Intimate Matters: A History of Sexuality in America* (New York: Harper & Row Publishers, 1988), 181.
9. "Passion and Power: An Introduction," in Kathy Peiss and Christian Simmons, ed., *Passion and Power: Sexuality in History* (Philadelphia: Temple University Press, 1989), 6.
10. Linda Brent, *Incidents in the Life of a Slave Girl: An Authentic Historical Narrative Describing the Horrors of Slavery as Experienced by Black Women* (New York: Harvest/Harcourt Brace Jovanovich Publishers, 1973), 53–54.
11. Ibid., 55.
12. Frantz Fanon, e.g., spoke of this practice from the perspective of the victims, noting along the way the manner in which these bodies are consumed piece by piece.
13. This is because the subjectivity of white bodies was harmed through an unreasonable assumption of superiority and the subjectivity of black bodies was warped through an assumption that they were inferior.
14. Judith Butler, *Bodies that Matter: On the Discursive Limits of "Sex"* (New York: Routledge, 1993), 1.
15. Fanon, *Black Skin, White Masks*, 159.
16. D'Emilio and Freedman, *Intimate Matters*, 86; R. W. Connell, "Bodies, Intellectuals, and the World Society," in Nick Waston and Sarah Cunningham-Berrley, ed., *Reframing the Body* (New York: Palgrave, 2001), 14.
17. Marcella Althaus-Reid, *Indecent Theology: Theological Perversions in Sex, Gender and Politics* (New York: Routledge, 2000), 88.
18. Wiesner-Hauls, *Christianity and Sexuality*, 238–239.
19. Ann-Janine Morey, *Religion and Sexuality in American* literature (New York: Cambridge University Press, 1992), 1.
20. Emilie M. Townes, *Breaking the Fine Rain of Death: African American Health Issues and a Womanist Ethic of Care* (New York: Continuum, 1998), 174.
21. Morey, *Religion and Sexuality*, 26.
22. David M. Carr, *The Erotic Word: Sexuality, Spirituality, and the Bible* (New York: Oxford University Press, 2003), 7.
23. Christine E. Gudorf, *Body, Sex, and Pleasure: Reconstructing Christian Sexual Ethics* (Cleveland, OH: The Pilgrim Press, 1994), 2–3.
24. Butler, *Bodies that Matter*, 178–179.
25. Nella Larsen, *Quicksand* with Introduction and notes by Thadious M. Davis (New York: Penguin Books, 2002), 114.
26. James Baldwin, *Go Tell It On the Mountain* (New York: Grosset and Dunlap/The University Library, 1953), 113.
27. Ibid., 269.
28. For an interesting and insightful discussion of the ramifications of the story of Ham in United States Race relations see: *Stephen R. Haynes, Noah's Curse: The Biblical Justification of American Slavery* (New York: Oxford University Press, 2002).

29. Baldwin, *Go Tell It On the Mountain*, 267.
30. Michael F. Lynch, "A Glimpse of the Hidden God: Dialectical Visions in Baldwin's *Go Tell It On the Mountain,*" in Trudier Harris, ed., *New Essays on Go Tell It On the Mountain* (NewYork: Cambridge University Press, 1996), 37–38.
31. Such a connection between sex(uality) and religion makes perfect sense, if Charles Long is correct in asserting that religion involves the body through a full array of structures, experiences, expressions, and behaviors in addition to modes of thought because it was through their bodies and the meaning of their bodies that the oppressed came to be understood and controlled in the context of modernity. The religion of the oppressed, in this case the religion of African Americans, entails an embodiment as they attempt, again turning to Long, to move from their second creation as objects of history back to their first creation as subjects, as fully human. See Charles H. Long, *Significations: Signs, Symbols, and Images in the Interpretation of Religion* (Philadelphia: Fortress Press, 1986), 7, 197.
32. Wiesner-Hauls, *Christianity and Sexuality*, 38.
33. Anthony Appiah, "Synthesis: For Racial Identities," in Amy Gutman and Anthony Appiah, *Color Consciousness: The Political Morality of Race* (Princeton: Princeton University Press, 1998), 95, 98.
34. James B. Nelson, *Body Theology* (Louisville, KY: Westminster/John Knox Press, 1992), 29.
35. Michael F. Lynch, "A Glimpse of the Hidden God: Dialectical Visions in Baldwin's *Go Tell It On the Mountain,*" in Harris, *New Essays on Go Tell It On the Mountain*, 39. Connected to this is the reality of sexuality as a construct, a sociopolitical, economic and culturally constructed something that has a history which often serves to make some uncomfortable in their skin in order to serve the needs of others. And when connected to additional markers such as race, its importance and power only increases.
36. Vivian M. May, "Ambivalent Narratives, Fragmented Selves: Performative Identities and the Mutability of Roles in James Baldwin's *Go Tell It On the Mountain,*" in Harris, *New Essays on Go Tell It On the Mountain.*
37. Michael F. Lynch, "A Glimpse of the Hidden God: Dialectical Visions in Baldwin's *Go Tell It On the Mountain,*" in Harris, *New Essays on Go Tell It On the Mountain*, 52–53.
38. (Maryknoll, NY: Orbis Books, 1999). Readers may also be interested in the critique I provide in *The Black Church in the Post-Civil Rights Era* (Maryknoll, NY: Orbis Books, 2002), chapter 5.
39. Kelly Brown Douglas, *Sexuality and the Black Church* (Maryknoll, NY: Orbis Books, 1999), 22–23.
40. Ibid., 7.
41. The problem of a stifled discourse is highlighted when one considers that even the blues, a musical form that seems to celebrate despised sexuality typically speaks of it in coded terms: Is "jellyroll" just a confectionery treat in the blues? While marketing requirements might have something to do with this at certain points in the history of blues recordings, there is still a sense in which implicit in this is sign of the non-discourse sex(uality) entails as a joy that on some level must be linguistically tamed. And when, in rap music, this taming of sex(uality) is not the case

'cause gangstas celebrate sex, the backlash against certain genres of explicit rap, albeit problematic genres, makes clear a discomfort with sex(uality) as public.

42. Douglas, *Sexuality and the Black Church*, 68.
43. Ibid., 114, 127.
44. Frederick C. Harris, *Something Within: Religion in African-American Political Activism* (NY: Oxford University Press, 1999), 169. This quotation and the next are taken from chapter five of my book *The Black Church*, 107.
45. Beverly Hall Lawrence, *Reviving the Spirit: A Generation of African Americans Goes Home to Church* (New York: Grove Press, 1996), 142–143. It would be interesting, but beyond the scope of this essay, to examine Goldie's attitude in light of Michael Dyson's theology of homoeroticism. See: Michael Eric Dyson, "Homotextualities: The Bible, Sexual Ethics, and the Theology of Homoeroticism." In Michael Eric Dyson, *Open Mike: Reflections on Philosophy, Race, Sex, Culture and Religion* (New York: Basic Civitas Books, 2003).
46. Douglas, *Sexuality and the Black Church*, 105.
47. Victor Anderson, *Beyond Ontological Blackness: An Essay on African American Religious and Cultural Criticism* (NewYork: Continuum, 1995), 21–50.
48. Mary Douglas, *Natural Symbols: Explorations in Cosmology* (NewYork: Routledge, 1996), 22, 69, 71.
49. Christine E. Gudorf, *Body, Sex, and Pleasure: Reconstructing Christian Sexual Ethics* (Cleveland, OH: The Pilgrim Press, 1994), 15.
50. Christine E. Gudorf uses this term when discussing the manner in which attention to what is sinful about sexuality teaches believers to avoid questionable actions, while failing to teach ways in which to construct productive relationships—those that involve sexual actions and those that do not. See Gudorf, *Body, Sex, and Pleasure*, 15.
51. Althaus-Reid, *Indecent Theology*,146.
52. Lisa Isherwood and Elizabeth Stuart, *Introducing Body Theology* (Sheffield, England: Sheffield Academic Press, 1998), 28.
53. Ibid., 31.
54. Ibid., 32.

Chapter Eight

1. Henry Louis Gates, Jr., "A Debate on Activism in Black Studies: A Call to Protect Academic Integrity from Politics," in Manning Marable, ed., *Dispatches from the Ebony Tower: Intellectuals Confront the African American Experience* (New York: Columbia University Press, 2000), 187.
2. I begin with theological concerns because theological studies is an area of interest for me, but also because I perceive it to be one of the more difficult areas for humanist thought in that it is commonly understood to be the restricted domain of Christian confessors. It should be noted, however, that a growing discomfort with the black church as normative within academic discussions of black religion expressed in various articles and books provides a theoretical opening for the discussion of humanism within the context of black religion (and the theological discourse connected to black religion).

3. While they may not discuss their work in this way, I would suggest philosophy as done by Lewis Gordon and William R. Jones, history as done by Juan Floyd-Thomas, ethics as discussed by Thandenka, community practice as described by Norm Allen are examples of how various dimensions of black humanist studies might develop.

I must acknowledge that my efforts with respect to a humanist theological discourse are an outgrowth of William R. Jones's earlier work in this area. See, for instance, William R. Jones, *Is God a White Racist?: A Preamble to Black Theology* (Boston: Beacon Press, 1999). Dr. Jones is certainly to be classified as one of the early figures in black humanist studies.

4. Some of the ideas expressed here were first sketched in "Black Is, Black Ain't: Victor Anderson, African American Theological Thought, and Identity," *Dialog: A Journal of Theology* Volume 43, No. 1 (Spring 2004): 53–61.

5. Recent examples include: Victor Anderson, *Beyond Ontological Blackness: An Essay on African American Religious and Cultural Criticism* (NewYork: Continuum, 1995); Dwight N. Hopkins, ed., *Black Faith and Public Talk: Critical Essays on James H. Cone's Black Theology and Black Power* (Maryknoll, NY : Orbis Books, 1999); Emilie M. Townes, *Breaking the Fine Rain of Death: African American Health Issues and a Womanist Ethic of Care* (NewYork: Continuum, 1998); Emilie M. Townes, ed., *A Troubling in My Soul: Womanist Perspectives on Evil & Suffering* (Maryknoll, NY: Orbis Books, 1993); Emilie M. Townes, ed., *Embracing the Spirit: Womanist Perspectives on Hope, Salvation, and Transformation* (Maryknoll, N.Y.: Orbis Books, 1997); Garth Kasimu Baker-Fletcher, *Xodus: An African American Male Journey* (Minneapolis: Fortress Press, 1996); Kelly Brown Douglas, *Sexuality and the Black Church: A Womanist Perspective* (Maryknoll, NY: Orbis Books, 1999).

6. Lewis Gordon, "Introduction: Black Existential Philosophy," 7; Roy D. Morrison II, "Self-Transformation in American Blacks: The Harlem Renaissance and Black Theology" in *Existence in Black*, 39–41.

7. Dwight Hopkins, *Down, Up, and Over: Slave Religion and Black Theology* (Minneapolis: Fortress Press, 2000), part two.

8. Paget Henry, "African And Afro-Caribbean Existential Philosophies, " in *Black Existence,* 15.

9. See Sharon Welch, *A Feminist Ethic of Risk*, revised edition (Minneapolis: Fortress Press, 2000), 177–180.

10. Houston A. Baker, Jr., *Afro-American Poetics: Revisions of Harlem and the Black Aesthetic* (Madison, WI: University of Wisconsin Press, 1988), 13.

11. I believe Victor Anderson speaks to similar concerns in *Beyond Ontological Blackness*.

12. I am grateful to Paula Cooey for this definition of essentialism.

13. Concerning the Nation of Islam on this see: Elijah Muhammad, *Message to the Blackman in America* (Chicago: Muhammad's Temple No. 2, 1965) and Elijah Muhammad, *Our Savior has Arrived* (Newport News, VA; United Brothers Communications Systems, nd). Robert Birt, "Existence, Identity, and Liberation," in Lewis R. Gordon, ed., *Existence in Black: An Anthology of Black Existential Philosophy* (New York: Routledge, 1997), 212.

14. Anderson, *Beyond Ontological Blackness*.

15. Hazel V. Carby, *Race Men* (Cambridge: Harvard University Press, 1999).

16. Douglas, *Sexuality and the Black Church*.

17. Stuart Hall, "What is This 'Black' in Black Popular Culture?" in a project by Michele Wallace and Gina Dent, eds., *Black Popular Culture* (Seattle: Bay Press, 1992), 29.

18. I found the following helpful in developing this perspective: Aldo Gargani's "Religious Experience as Event and Interpretation," in Jacques Derrida and Gianni Vattimo, ed., *Religion* (Stanford: Stanford University Press, 1998), 111–135. I also see this perspective as related to common understandings of Michel Foucault's take on religion. See for an example of this: Jeremy R. Carrette, editor, "Prologue to a confession of the Flesh," in *Religion and Culture: Michel Foucault* (New York: Routledge, 1999), 1–47. At this point in my work on a black Theology of Immanence, my concern with religion involves function and form as opposed to traditional categories of belief. I only address these, such as God, as the need presents itself.

19. I find my colleague's, Paula Cooey, discussion of religious experience in relation to the body extremely helpful. See: Paula M. Cooey, *Religious Imagination and the Body: A Feminist Analysis.* (New York: Oxford University Press, 1999). For examples of this internal versus. external critique and the subtle consequences of this dichotomy see the debate between James Cone and William Jones (particularly Cone's response as outlined in *God of the Oppressed* [New York: Seabury Press, 1975]). Also see, Major Jones, *The Color of G.O.D.* (Macon, GA : Mercer, c1987). Dwight Hopkins also demonstrates this tendency in *Introducing Black Theology of Liberation* (Maryknoll, NY: Orbis Books, 1999) in that the work of Wilmore and Long do not significantly impact the Black theology project's methodological framework and content.

20. Cone, *God of the Oppressed,* 91.

21. Even so, the theological discourse I suggest here is not suspect because of this negative understanding of ideology. There are also definitions that paint ideology in positive terms. See Charles Long, "Human Centers . . . ," in *Significations*, 74–78.

22. Cone, *God of the Oppressed* ,102–103.

23. Additional work in a black humanist theological discourse will need to consider the work of liberal theologians and the ways in which they addressed issues of religious experience, etc.

Chapter Nine

1. This chapter is a revised version of "Black Theology, Black Bodies, and Pedagogy," in *CrossCurrents*, Fiftieth Anniversary Issues, Volume 50, Nos. 1–2 (Spring/ Summer 2000): 196–202. A few of the ideas are also developed in "Facing Competing Claims: Thoughts on a Theory of Theological Discourse" *Theological Education*, volume 38, Number 2 (2002): 87–95.

2. Although I refuse to believe students bring nothing of merit to the educational process, if Charles Long is correct, such a conversation is important because "religion" tends to be "the only subject matter that is not in continuity with other forms of subject matter in previous secondary formal education. . . . This means"

according to Long, "that students do not really know what to expect when they come to a religion course on the college level. Most students' understanding or knowledge of religion is held, whether positively or negatively, in a rather personal manner; and this is usually related to some experience and meaning given to religion by their families and communities. For the most part, their notions of religion have never been subjected to any form of critical thought or reflection." Charles Long, "The University, the Liberal Arts, and the Teaching and Study of Religion," in Frank E. Reynolds and Sheryl L. Burkhalter, ed., *Beyond the Classics?: Essays in Religious Studies and Liberal Education* (Atlanta: Scholars Press, 1990), 35.

3. This use of the term ritual is heavily indebted to Ritual Studies, particularly the early work of Ronald Grimes. Grimes, e.g., extends the range of ritual to include what is typically understood as "ordinary" moments and activities. In his words: "I suggest that ritual pervades more of our life than just an isolated realm designated 'religious.' It suffuses our biogenetic, psychosocial, political, economic, and artistic lives as well. . . . Often we begin to speak of ritual in far too lofty a way by referring to ultimacy, sacredness, awe, sacrifice, or eternity, or in too specific and normative a way by confessing our faith regarding specific personages or religious traditions. As a result, we sometimes unwittingly disincarnate ourselves from our own bodies, our own present, and our own ordinariness." See: Ronald Grimes, *Beginnings in Ritual Studies* (Washington, DC: University Press of America, Inc., 1982). Ritual, then, according to Grimes involves complex or thick and repeated activities in founded places all of which involve in some manner the human body. This definition is useful for my purposes in that it is a general definition that allows for a wide gaze. Ritualizing, accordingly, is not confined to the work of formal structures of worship, but are open to change, alteration, and replacement (58–60).

4. William G. Doty, *Mythography: The Study of Myths and Rituals* (Birmingham: The University of Alabama Press, 1986), 108.

5. Grimes, *Beginnings in Ritual Studies*, 87.

6. Ibid., 87.

7. Ibid., 99.

8. Ibid., 87.

9. I have in mind the appeal to an awareness of the body provided by bell hooks, informed by the work of those in Ritual Studies. See: bell hooks, *Teaching to Transgress: Education as the Practice of Freedom* (New York: Routledge, 1994).

10. Lawrence Sullivan, " 'Seeking an End to the Primary Text' or 'Putting an End to the Text as Primary,' " in Frank E. Reynolds and Sheryl L. Burkhalter, ed., *Beyond the Classics?: Essays in Religious Studies and Liberal Education* (Atlanta: Scholars Press, 1990), 44.

11. William G. Doty, *Mythography: The Study of Myths and Rituals,* , 100.

12. Ibid., 101, 108.

13. Lawrence Sullivan, " 'Seeking an End to the Primary Text' or 'Putting an End to the Text as Primary,' " in Frank E. Reynolds and Sheryl L. Burkhalter, ed., *Beyond the Classics?: Essays in Religious Studies and Liberal Education* (Atlanta: Scholars Press, 1990), 51, 53.

14. Doty, *Mythography*, 115.

15. Ibid., 79.

Selected Bibliography

Allen, Jr., Norm, editor. *Personal Paths to Humanism* (Amherst, NY: Prometheus Books, 2003).

Allen, Jr., Norm, editor. *African American Humanism: An Anthology* (Amherst, NY: Prometheus Books, 1992).

Althaus-Reid, Marcella. *Indecent Theology: Theological Perversions in Sex, Gender and Politics* (New York: Routledge, 2000).

Anderson, Victor. *Beyond Ontological Blackness: An Essay on African American Religious and Cultural Criticism* (New York: Continuum Press, 1995).

Baker, Houston A. *Afro-American Poetics: Revisions of Harlem and the Black Aesthetic* (Madison, WI: University of Wisconsin Press, 1988).

Baldwin, James. *The Fire Next Time* (New York: Dell Books, 1962).

Berlin, Ira et al. *Remembering Slavery: African Americans Talk About Their Personal Experiences of Slavery and Freedom* (New York: The New Press/ Washington, D.C.: Library of Congress, 1998).

Bruce, Steve et al. *The Rapture of Politics: the Christian Right as the United States Approaches the Year 2000* (New Brunswick, NJ: Transaction Publishers, 1995).

Butler, Judith. *Bodies that Matter: On the Discursive Limits of "Sex"* (New York: Routledge, 1993).

Camus, Albert. *The Rebel: An Essay on Man in Revolt* (New York: Vintage International, 1991).

Caplan, Pat, Editor. *The Cultural Construction of Sexuality* (New York: Tavistock Publications, 1987).

Capps, Walter H. *The New Religious Right: Piety, Patriotism, and Politics* (Columbia: University of South Carolina, 1990).

Carr, David M. *The Erotic Word: Sexuality, Spirituality, and the Bible* (New York: Oxford University Press, 2003).

Carrette, Jeremy R., Editor. *Religion and Culture: Michel Foucault* (New York: Routledge, 1999).

Cooey, Paula M. *Religious Imagination and the Body: A Feminist Analysis* (New York: Oxford University Press, 1999).

Cruse, Harold. "Jews and Negroes in the Communist Party," in *The Crisis of the Negro Intellectual: A Historical Analysis of the Failure of Black Leadership* (New York: William Morrow and Company/Quill, 1967, 1984).

Culpitt, Don. *After God: The Future of Religion* (New York: Basic Books, 1997).

D'Emilio and Estelle B. Freedman. *Intimate Matters: A History of Sexuality in America* (New York: Harper & Row Publishers, 1988).

Dietrich, John H. *What If The World Went Humanist?: Ten Sermons*, selected by Mason Olds (Yellow Springs, OH: Fellowship of Religious Humanists, 1989).

Doty, William G. *Mythography: The Study of Myths and Rituals* (Birmingham: The University of Alabama Press, 1986).

Douglas, Mary. *Natural Symbols: Explorations in Cosmology* (New York: Routledge, 1996).

Douglas, Kelly Brown. *Sexuality and the Black Church* (Maryknoll, NY: Orbis Books, 1999).

Dyson, Michael Eric. *Open Mike: Reflections on Philosophy, Race, Sex, Culture and Religion* (New York: Basic Civitas Books, 2003).

Dyson, Michael Eric. *Holler If You Hear Me: Searching for Tupac Shakur* (New York: Basic Civitas Books, 2001).

Ellingson, Stephen and M. Christian Green, editors. *Religion and Sexuality in Cross-Cultural Perspective* (New York: Routledge, 2002).

Fanon, Frantz. *Black Skin, White Masks* (New York: Grove Press Inc., 1967).

Forman, James. "Corrupt Black preachers," in *The Making of Black Revolutionaries* (Washington, DC: Open Hand Publishing, Inc., 1985).

Foucault, Michel. *Discipline and Punish: The Birth of the Prison* (New York: Vintage Books, 1979).

Gardella, Peter. *Innocent Ecstasy: How Christianity Gave America an Ethic of Sexual Pleasure* (New York: Oxford University Press, 1985).

Girard, Rene. *Violence and the Sacred*. Translated by Patrick Gregory (Baltimore: The Johns Hopkins University Press, 1977).

Gordon, Lewis, editor. *Existence in Black: An Anthology of Black Existential Philosophy* (New York: Routledge, 1997).

Grimes, Ronald. *Beginnings in Ritual Studies* (Washington, DC: University Press of America, Inc., 1982).

Gudorf, Christine E. *Body, Sex, and Pleasure: Reconstructing Christian Sexual Ethics* (Cleveland, OH: The Pilgrim Press, 1994).

Harding, Susan Friend. *The Book of Jerry Falwell: Fundamentalist Language and Politics* (Princeton: Princeton University Press, 2000).

Harrison, Hubert. *The Negro and the Nation* (New York: Cosmo-Advocate Publishing Co., 1917).

Harris, David A. *Profiles in Injustice: Why Racial Profiling Cannot Work* (New York: The New Press, 2002).

Haynes, *Stephen R. Noah's Curse: The Biblical Justification of American Slavery* (New York: Oxford University Press, 2002).

Heywood, Ian and Barry Sandywell, editors. *Interpreting Visual Culture: Explorations in the Hermeneutics of the Visual* (New York: Routledge, 1999).

Hooks, Bell. *Teaching to Transgress: Education as the Practice of Freedom* (New York: Routledge, 1994).

Hopkins, Dwight. *Down, Up, and Over: Slave Religion and Black Theology* (Minneapolis: Fortress Press, 2000).

Hughes, Langston. *Good Morning Revolution: Uncollected Writings of Social Protest by Langston Hughes*, Introduction by Faith Berry (New York: Carol Publishing Group).

Humanist Manifestos I and II (Buffalo, NY: Prometheus, 1973).

James, William. *The Meaning of Truth: A Sequel to Pragmatism* (Cambridge, MA: Harvard University Press, 1975).

Johnson, Stephen D. and Joseph B. Tamney, editors, *The Political Role of Religion in the United States* (Boulder, CO: Westview Press, 1986).

Jones, William R. *Is God a White Racist?: A Preamble to Black Theology* (Boston: Beacon Press, 1999).

Kelley, Robin D. G. "Comrades, Praise Gawd for Lenin and Them!: Ideology and Culture Among Black Communities in Alabama, 1930–1935," *Science and Society*, Vol. 52, No. 1, Spring 1988.

Kurtz, Paul, editor, *Moral Problems in Contemporary Society* (Englewood Cliffs, NJ: Prentice-Hall, Inc., 1969).

Kurtz, Paul. *Forbidden Fruit: The Ethics of Humanism* (Buffalo, NY: Prometheus Books, 1988).

Lamont, Corliss. *The Philosophy of Humanism* (New York: Frederick Ungar Publishing, Co., 1965

Lawrence, Bruce B. *Defenders of God: The Fundamentalist Revolt Against the Modern Age* (Columbia: University of South Carolina Press, 1989).

Lienesch, Michael. *Redeeming America: Piety & Politics in the New Christian Right* (Chapel Hill: The University of North Carolina Press, 1993).

Levy, Eugene. *James Weldon Johnson: Black Leader, Black Voice* (Chicago: The University of Chicago Press).

Long, Charles H. *Significations: Signs, Symbols, and Images in the Interpretation of Religion* (Philadelphia: Fortress Press, 1986).

Marable, Manning. *Dispatches from the Ebony Tower: Intellectuals Confront the African American Experience* (New York: Columbia University Press, 2000).

Marsden, George M. *Understanding Fundamentalism and Evangelicalism* (Grand Rapids, MI: William B. Eerdmans Publishing Company, 1991).

Mays, Benjamin E. *The Negro's God as Reflected in His Literature* (New York: Atheneum, 1973).

May, Henry F. *The Enlightenment in America* (New York: Oxford University Press, 1976).

Meeks, Kenneth. *Driving While Black* (New York: Broadway Books, 2000).

Meyer, Donald H. "Secular Transcendence: The American Religious Humanists," *American Quarterly*, Vol. 34, No. 5 (Winter 1982): 524–542.

Morey, Ann-Janine. *Religion and Sexuality in American Literature* (New York: Cambridge University Press, 1992).

Morrison-Reed, Mark D. *Black Pioneers in a White Denomination*, 3rd edition (Boston: Skinner House Books, 1994).

Nelson, James B. *Body Theology* (Louisville, KY: Westminster/John Knox Press, 1992).

Newton, Huey P. *To Die For The People: The Writings of Huey P. Newton*, edited by Toni Morrison (New York: Writers and Readers Publishing, Inc., 1995).

Olds, Mason."What Is Religious Humanism?" *Free Inquiry*, Vol. 16, No. 4 (Fall 1996): 13.

Painter, Nell Irvin. *The Narrative of Hosea Hudson: His Life as a Negro Communist in the South* (Cambridge, MA: Harvard University Press, 1979).

Payne, Daniel Alexander. "Daniel Payne's Protestation of Slavery," *Lutheran Herald and Journal of the Franckean Synod* (August 1, 1839).

Peiss, Kathey and Christian Simmons, editors. *Passion and Power: Sexuality in History* (Philadelphia: Temple University Press, 1989).

Pinn, Anthony B. *Terror and Triumph: The Nature of Black Religion* (Minneapolis: Fortress Press, 2003).

Pinn, Anthony B, editor. *By These Hands: A Documentary History of African American Humanism* (New York: New York University Press, 2001).

Pinn, Anthony B. *Varieties of African American Religious Experience* (Minneapolis: Fortress Press, 1998).

Pinn, Anthony B. *Why, Lord?: Suffering and Evil in Black Theology* (New York: Continuum, 1995).

Rabil, Jr., Albert. *Renaissance Humanism: Foundations, Forms, and Legacy, Volume 3—Humanism and the Disciplines* (Philadelphia: University of Pennsylvania Press, 1988).

Redding, J. Saunders. *On Being Negro in America* (New York: The Bobbs-Merrill Company, Inc., 1951).

Redding, J. Saunders. Edited with an Introduction by Faith Berry, *A Scholar's Conscience: Selected Writings of J. Saunders Redding, 1942–1977* (Louisville: The University Press of Kentucky, 1992).

Reynolds, Frank E., And Sheryl L. Burkhalter, editors. *Beyond the Classics?: Essays in Religious Studies and Liberal Education* (Atlanta: Scholars Press, 1990).

Sartre, Jean-Paul. *Existentialism and Human Emotions* (New York: Carol Publishing Group, 1957, 1990).

Seale, Bobby. *Seize the Time: The Story of the Black Panther Party and Huey P. Newton* (Baltimore: Black Classic Press, 1991/New York: Random House, 1970).

Townes, Emilie M. *Breaking the Fine Rain of Death: African American Health Issues and a Womanist Ethics of Care* (New York: Continuum, 1998).

Walker, Alice. "The only reason you want to go to heaven is that you have been driven out of your mind (off your land and out of your lover's arms): clear seeing, inherited religion and reclaiming the pagan self," *On The Issues*, Vol. VI, No. Two, Spring 1997.

Wallace, Michelle and Gina Dent, editors. *Black Popular Culture* (Seattle: Bay Press, 1992).

Welch, Sharon. *Sweet Dreams in America: Making Ethics and Spirituality Work* (New York: Routledge, 1999).

Welch, Sharon. *An Ethic of Risk* (Minneapolis: Fortress Press, 1999).

Wiesner-Hauls, Meery E. *Christianity and Sexuality in the Early Modern World: Regulating Desire, Reforming Practice* (New York: Routledge, 2000).

Wilmore, Gayraud. *Black Religion and Black Radicalism: An Interpretation of the Religious History of Afro-American People*, 2nd edition (Maryknoll, NY: Orbis Books, 1983).

Wright, Richard. *The Outsider* (New York: HarperPerennial, 1993).

Wright, Richard. *Black Boy* (New York: Harper & Row, Publishers, 1966).

Index

AAH (African Americans for Humanism), 38
Abortion, 42, 51
ACLU (American Civil Liberties Union), 47
Africa, 97, 102
African American humanism: and afterlife, 58–60; and Black power movement, 29–33, 36, 37; and communism, 27–29; conversion to, 27, 30–31; as hermeneutic, 5–6, 8, 10, 61–62, 77, 83, 115n.10; historical development of, 8, 9, 10, 11–38; and Nimrod, 2–7; organizational force in, 33–38; Pinn's personal reflections on, xiii–xxiii; as praxis, 6, 9, 10, 39–40, 115n.10; principles of, 7, 65–67, 119–20n.11; and rap music, 62, 66–76, 122n.6; and rejection of God concept, xxi, 7, 8–9, 123n.30; and slaves, 16–18; and Theology of Immanence, 103, 106, 130n.18; twentieth-century developments in, 18–38, *see also* Black humanist studies; Body; Sex(uality)
African American Humanist Declaration, 38
African American Studies, 101, 102, 103
African Americans: assumed inferiority of, 79–80, 126n.13; essentialist notions of identity of, 105; "negro" as term for, 6; as Other, 82, 84, 85; struggles

of, for full humanity, 5, *see also* Body; Sex(uality); Slave trade; Slavery
African Americans for Humanism (AAH), 38
African diaspora, 102
African gods, 97
African Methodist Episcopal (AME) Church, xv–xix, 94
Afterlife, *see* Heaven and afterlife
Agnostic humanism, 120n.11, 120n.18
Agnosticism, 29
Alabama, 51
Allen, Norm, 37–38, 129n.3
AME Church, xv–xix, 94
American Civil Liberties Union (ACLU), 47
American Humanist Association, 7
Anderson, Victor, 95, 105
Apocalypse, 52–53
Appeal (Walker), 5
Appiah, Anthony, 91
Aquinas, Thomas, 125n.4
Arrested Development, 71–72
Atheism, xi–xii, xxi–xxii, 8–9, 28, 47, 115n.11, 120n.18
Atlanta University, 22
Augustine, St., 4, 56–57, 88

Babel, 3–4
Bakhtin, Mikhail, 64
Baldwin, James, xvi, 19–21, 90–92
Baltimore, 94
Baptist Church, xiv, 37, 72
Baraka, Amiri Imamu, 11
Becoming, 66
Bell, Derrick, 77

9 781403 966247